Philosophy of Religion
Religion
A Beginner's Guide

ONEWORLD BEGINNER'S GUIDES combine an original, inventive, and engaging approach with expert analysis on subjects ranging from art and history to religion and politics, and everything in between. Innovative and affordable, books in the series are perfect for anyone curious about the way the world works and the big ideas of our time.

Philosophy of Religion
A Beginner's Guide

Charles Taliaferro

ONEWORLD

OXFORD

A Oneworld Paperback Original

Published by Oneworld Publications 2009

ISBN 978–1–85168–650–6

Typeset by Jayvee, Trivandrum, India
Cover design by fatfacedesign.co.uk
Printed and bound in Great Britain by TJ International, Padstow

Oneworld Publications
185 Banbury Road
Oxford OX2 7AR
England
www.oneworld-publications.com

Mixed Sources
Product group from well-managed
forests and other controlled sources
www.fsc.org Cert no. SGS-COC-2482
© 1996 Forest Stewardship Council

Learn more about Oneworld. Join our mailing list to
find out about our latest titles and special offers at:

www.oneworld-publications.com

Contents

Preface

Is there a God? Is the cosmos created? Is evil compatible with an all-powerful, all-knowing, all-good creator? Can we experience God? How can we tell whether religious experiences are reliable? What is the relationship between religions? How are their different concepts of the sacred and of ultimate reality related? How should we assess the value of religious practices like prayer, meditation, worship, pilgrimages, and the love of God and neighbor? Do they make sense? Could we survive death? What is the relationship between religion and science? Between religion and morality? What should be the relationship between religion and politics?

These are only some of the questions that define the philosophy of religion. Philosophically reflecting on religion is not an abstract theoretical enterprise of interest only to the professional philosopher. It also has clear relevance to contemporary life, requiring philosophical engagement with the beliefs and practices of the majority of the world population. Only 550 million of the world's 6.7 billion people claim to be non-religious, secular atheists, agnostics, or skeptics. In the 1960s it was thought by some sociologists that world religions would severely atrophy in the coming decades, but quite the reverse has taken place (Berger 1997, 974; Stark 2006).

The philosophy of religion provides an exciting point of contact between different cultures. Its themes bear on both Eastern and Western thought, and the relationship between the Northern and Southern Hemispheres. I have been part of delegations of philosophers from the West to Russia and China which have taken part in sustained, rich exchanges on the subject of philosophy of religion. There, rather than being dismissed as an opiate of the people or as of only marginal historical interest, as it was in Soviet and Maoist days, religious traditions are now taken seriously as sources for contemporary thinking not only about God but about value theory and the philosophy of language and culture. This is a far cry from the first philosophy conference I attended as an undergraduate student: the Fourteenth World Congress of Philosophy held in Bulgaria in 1973, before the collapse of Soviet power. At the philosophy of religion session, a Chinese philosopher gave an enthusiastic report on the Chinese government's success in secularizing Mongolia. Now, Chinese scholars spend time not on thinking about the social engineering of religious doubt or belief, but on investigating the nature and credibility of religion in the context of the democratic culture being fostered on the campuses of the great Chinese universities.

Philosophy of religion is one of the most intellectually exciting areas of philosophy, for it touches on virtually *every* other area of philosophy, from the philosophy of space and time, of science, to ethics, logic, and epistemology.

Finally, the philosophy of religion speaks directly to the meaning of life. The teachings of the world religions may seem to some to be antiquated and irrelevant, but a moment's exploration of religion reveals them to be *radically* important – should one or more of them be true. In the 1970s and 1980s it was fashionable for academic philosophers to dismiss questions about the meaning of life. Life is too fragmented to have a meaning, at least a meaning we can discern. But we persist in asking about the *meaning* or *significance* of our life and therefore about the possible role and truth of religion. Buddhism holds that the concept of the self as a substantial, concrete individual enduring over time and a life built on the pursuit of desire is deeply problematic. Christianity (in its traditional form) holds that we are enduring substantial beings (sometimes thought of as embodied souls) who are made such that our deepest desires for fulfillment are found in relationship with God. If Buddhism is right, the meaning of our ego-driven, desire-ridden lives contains deep illusions. If Christianity is right, the cosmos is created and the arena of a fierce conflict between good and evil, and each person's well-being depends ultimately on an order of loving desire (what Augustine referred to as the *ordo amoris* or the order of love).

This *Beginner's Guide* will introduce you to the main themes of contemporary philosophy of religion. It will explore the five major world religions – Judaism, Christianity, Islam, Hinduism, and Buddhism – and religious pluralism and the secular challenge to religious traditions.

Before we begin, it is worth pausing to reflect on the emotions and attitudes that can come into play in philosophizing about religion.

Recent books like Daniel Dennett's *Breaking the Spell*, Sam Harris's *Letter to a Christian Nation* and *The End of Faith*, and Richard Dawkins's *The God Delusion* seem, in my view, to be both over-confident in their assertions and very one-sided in their approach to religion. The books by Dawkins and Dennett will be taken seriously in what follows, for they contain important arguments. They have done a great deal of good by bringing the topic of religion to the fore in public discourse. I could not agree more with Daniel Dennett's claim that

It is high time that we subject religion as a global phenomenon to the most intensive multidisciplinary research we can muster, calling on the best minds on the planet. Why? Because religion is too important for us to remain ignorant about. It affects not just our social, political, and economic conflicts, but the very meanings we find in our lives. For many people, probably a majority of the people on Earth, nothing matters more than religion. For this reason, it is imperative that we learn as much as we can about it.

(Dennett 2006, 14, 15)

But though I commend his counsel and many of his insights, I hope this book will be more generous than his, Harris's, and Dawkins's to both 'believers' and 'skeptics'. I will not, for example, advance brazen and I believe unsupported charges that either religious belief or skepticism about religion is ignorant, hateful, and greedy, as does Harris (2004, 226). A spirit of generosity is called for in the philosophy of religion because there are good arguments for almost every position. There are good reasons for theism as well as for atheism, good reasons for being a Christian, and good reasons for being a Buddhist, and good reasons for being a skeptic.

I propose what may be called 'the golden rule in philosophy': that one should treat other philosophies as one would like one's own to be treated. Unfortunately, this golden rule is not always followed. There are, for example, two important philosophical texts currently in print that refer to Christian philosophers of religion as 'Christian apologists'. There is nothing wrong with being an apologist, which technically means someone who advocates or defends some position, but for most philosophers an 'apologist' is a *missionary* or *preacher*, not someone undertaking honest philosophical inquiry. Would the authors of these texts – who happen to be naturalists (people who believe that there is no God and that only nature exits) – like to be labeled 'apologists for naturalism'? They certainly do not use the term 'apologist' when referring to themselves or their fellow naturalists and that is a good reason for them not to refer to 'the opposition' as apologists. It is more respectful – and more fruitful – to describe views with which you disagree in the way you would like your own convictions to be addressed: fairly, respectfully, and with sympathy.

Closely related to a philosophical golden rule, I propose one more practice: 'philosophical good-Samaritanism', the practice of going to someone's aid when in need. At a North American philosophy conference I witnessed a vibrant, ideal exchange between a very prominent theist, Eleonore Stump, and the well-known philosopher David Lewis. Stump had developed a nuanced, philosophically interesting concept of the Christian belief in the incarnation. She faced a series of trenchant objections. Almost at the very end, Professor Lewis raised his hand and said something like: 'Although I am an atheist, and I do not believe in the Incarnation, *if I did think there was a God*, then an Incarnation might occur in the following way ...' I do not recall the detailed alternative that Lewis articulated that afternoon (an account that complemented Stump's theory), but his intellectual generosity and openness were impressive. This was not by any mean an isolated event (professional philosophers almost routinely seek to develop arguments and objections against their own views), but the Lewis–Stump exchange took place with particular grace and good humor in an otherwise quite uncomfortable lecture hall.

Such generosity is so much more appealing than the sometimes martial way in which debate can be carried out when people set out to *destroy*, *attack*, *undermine*, *defend* (etc.) this or that position. In my experience, philosophy is best done among groups where there is an authentic spirit of friendship or camaraderie. And it is in that spirit that one should not take too much delight in opposing a fellow philosopher's position; rather, from time to time one should also positively repair or reconstruct the work of others, even those with whom one profoundly disagrees. I suggest, then, that good philosophical inquiry, especially in matters of religion, should include cooperative assistance.

My final point in this introduction concerns a practical matter. Whether you are reading this book alone or in a large class, find a friend (or two) who welcomes arguments and good-humored, open-ended dialogue. Getting started in philosophy is like learning a language: practice is essential. On your own, you may read closely or listen well to lectures, and even cultivate an internal dialogue on the issues (Plato defined 'thinking' as 'a dialogue within the soul'). But after more than twenty years as a college professor, I am convinced that nothing can replace the enormous value and excitement of ongoing exchange with a friend who listens sympathetically, challenges your insights, and contributes fresh observations of her or his own.

Acknowledgements

I am immensely grateful to Martha Jay for proposing that I undertake this guide, and to Mike Harpley for his guidance in completing the work, as well as to an anonymous reader for Oneworld Publications. Without the superb, professional help of Tricia Little in preparing the manuscript, this work would not have been completed. I am also deeply grateful for editorial direction from David Mills as well as the assistance from Aaron Stauffer, and I thank Anthony Nanson for his excellent copyediting. I thank Kate Smith for her excellent work in the final formation of this text. I am grateful (as always) to Elsa Marty and Graham Martin for their superb comments on an early draft of this book. This book is very much a reflection of invaluable conversations with students in philosophy of religion at St Olaf College, the University of Notre Dame, the University of Massachusetts, and Brown University. It is dedicated to Ed Langerak, an ideal colleague, outstanding teacher, and mentor. It is also dedicated with affection and respect to eight scholars I have had the honor of working with in the past ten years: Paul Draper, Jil Evans, Stewart Goetz, Paul Griffiths, Michel LeGall, Chad Meister, Paul Reasoner, and Alison Teply. I have learned more from collaboration with these fine scholars than I can possibly say.

1

Philosophical inquiry into religion

The word 'philosophy' is derived from the Greek word for 'love of wisdom'. In the West and East, the love of wisdom first took shape largely in response to mayhem and crisis. The ancient Greek philosopher Socrates (470–399 BCE) was a veteran of a defeated army. He served Athens in the war against Sparta (the Peloponnesian War), a war that Athens provoked, and lost decisively. In ancient China, Confucius (551–479 BCE) developed his philosophy of education, virtue, and rites during a period of widespread violence fomented by warlords; in addition to being among China's first philosophers, Confucius probably served as an officer of the law. Both developed what we call 'philosophy' in a period of cultural and political instability, for in such times there grows a desire to know the answers to questions like: What is justice? What is our duty to our family and our city? What is courage? Friendship? For what reasons – if any – should I be willing to die? Is it ever right to kill another person? What are the gods and what role should they play in our lives? Is there life beyond death? Should we honor our ancestors? If so, how?

For Socrates and Confucius, the pursuit of wisdom involves addressing basic questions about the nature and value of life. As a working definition of philosophy, I suggest a two-fold distinction. *To have a philosophy* is simply to have a view of reality and value. Given this definition, almost all reflective persons are philosophers, even if a person's philosophy happens to be quite haphazard and incomplete. Apart from this general definition, *to practice philosophy* is to do what Socrates and Confucius did: to investigate the ways in which reason and experience justify views about justice, the divine, the meaning of birth, life, and death, and so on. The practice of philosophy is not, then, simply to entertain different views of reality; it's to engage in disciplined inquiry. Such inquiry often involves close attention to the meaning of terms; Confucius believed that one of the most important rules of thought is the careful use of words and Socrates argued that a source of great confusion and conflict is our failure to understand the terms we use. Philosophers, then, seek to clarify our views of reality, values, language, and to carefully consider what we may or should believe and feel, and how we should act. Some philosophers have been profound skeptics, arguing that humanity is deeply ignorant about reality, but the majority of philosophers have advanced competing theories and constructive arguments that call for engaging reflection.

The English term 'religion' is derived from the Latin term for 'to bind' and was used originally to refer to what bound people together in their beliefs about the gods and the practices they followed. Today, the word covers the five major world religions – Judaism, Christianity, Islam, Hinduism, and Buddhism – and more. Let us consider an overview of these religions and then examine several possible definitions of 'religion'. In addition to the five world religions, there are numerous other significant traditions that are customarily identified as religious. These include Confucianism, Taoism, Baha'ism, and Zoroastrianism, as well as the diverse African and Native American traditions. These will not all be bypassed in this *Beginner's Guide*, but for now let us consider the larger religions.

The three monotheistic religions

Three of these traditions are called *Abrahamic* because they trace their history back to the Hebrew patriarch Abraham (often dated to the twentieth or twenty-first century BCE). Judaism, Christianity, and Islam each see themselves as rooted in Abrahamic faith, as displayed in the Hebrew Bible, the Christian Old Testament (essentially the Hebrew Bible) and New Testament, and the Qur'an. 'Theism' has been since the seventeenth century the common term in English to refer to their central concept of God. According to the classical forms of these faiths, God is the one and sole God (they are *monotheistic* as opposed to *polytheistic*) who created and sustains the cosmos. God either created the cosmos out of nothing (*ex nihilo*) or it has always existed but depends for its existence upon God's conserving, creative will. (Some Islamic philosophers have claimed that the cosmos has always existed as God's sustained creation, but the great majority of philosophers in these three traditions have held that the cosmos had a beginning.) Creation from nothing means that that which is created was not created by God shaping or using anything external to God. The cosmos depends upon God's conserving, continuous will the way light depends on a source or a song depends on a singer. If the source of the light goes out or the singer stops singing, the light and song cease. Traditionally, the creation is not thought of as a thing that an agent might fashion and then abandon; the idea that God might make creation and then neglect it the way a person might make a machine and then abandon it is utterly foreign to theism.

In these religions, God is said to exist *necessarily*, not *contingently*. God exists in God's self, not as the creation of some greater being (a super-God) or force of nature. God is also not a mode of something more fundamental, the way a wave is a mode of the sea or a dance is a mode of movement. The cosmos, in contrast, exists *contingently* but not *necessarily* – it might not have existed at all; God's existence is unconditional insofar as it does not depend upon any external conditions, whereas the cosmos is conditional.

Theists hold that God is, rather, a *substantial reality*: a being not explainable in terms that are more fundamental than itself. God is without parts, that is, not an aggregate or compilation of things. Theists describe God as holy or sacred, a reality that is of unsurpassable greatness. God is therefore also thought of as perfectly good, beautiful, all-powerful (omnipotent), present everywhere (omnipresent), and all-knowing (omniscient). God is without origin and without end, and everlasting or eternal. Because of all this, God is worthy of worship and morally sovereign (worthy of obedience). Finally, God is manifested in human history; God's nature and will are displayed in the tradition's sacred scriptures.

Arguably, the most central attribute of God in the Abrahamic traditions is *goodness*. The idea that God is not good or the fundamental source of goodness would be akin to the idea of a square circle – an utter contradiction.

Theists in these traditions differ on some of the divine attributes. Some, for example, claim that God knows all future events with certainty, whereas others argue that no being (including God) can have such knowledge. Some theists believe that God transcends both space and time altogether, while other theists hold that God pervades the spatial world and is temporal (there is before, during, and after for God). We will consider some of these differences in the next chapter. But it is largely in their views of God's special revelation that the three monotheistic traditions diverge.

In Judaism, God's principal manifestation was in leading the people of Israel out of bondage in Egypt to the Promised Land (Canaan) as recounted in Exodus. This 'saving event' is commemorated perennially in the yearly observation of Passover. The tradition places enormous value on community life, a life displayed in the Hebrew Bible as a covenant between God and the people of Israel. The more traditional representatives of Judaism, especially the Orthodox, adopt a strict reading of what they take to be the historic meaning of the Hebrew scripture as secured in the early stages of its formation. Other groups, like the Conservative and Reformed, treat scripture as authoritative but do not depend on a specific, historically defined interpretation of that scripture. Although there is some lively disagreement about the extent to which Judaism affirms an afterlife of individuals, Judaism has historically affirmed there is an afterlife.

Christians accept the Hebrew scriptures and Judaism's understanding of God's action in history, and expand them in holding that God became incarnate as Jesus Christ (a person who has both divine and human natures), whose birth, life, teaching, miracles, suffering, death, and resurrection are the principle means by which God delivers creation from its sin (moral and spiritual evil) and devastation. As part of its teaching about the incarnation, Christianity holds that while God is one, God is constituted by three persons in a supreme, singular unity called the Trinity (to be discussed briefly in chapter 5). Traditional Christianity asserts that through God's loving mercy and justice, individual persons are not annihilated at death, but either enjoy an afterlife of heaven or endure one of hell. Some Christians have been and are *universalists*, holding that ultimately God will triumph over all evil and there will be universal salvation for all people, though a greater part of the tradition holds that God will not violate the free will of creatures and that if persons seek to reject God, then those persons will be everlastingly separate from God.

Some unity of Christian belief and practice was gradually achieved in the course of developing various creeds (the word comes from the Latin *credo*, 'I believe', with which the creeds used in worship traditionally began) that defined Christian faith in formal terms. The Nicene Creed, most of which was written and approved in the third century, is the most famous and most widely shared of these. At the heart of traditional Christianity is a ritual of initiation (baptism) and the Eucharist, a rite that re-enacts or recalls Christ's self-offering through sharing blessed bread and wine (sometimes called *communion* or *mass*). What unity Christianity achieved was broken, however, in the eleventh century with the split between the Western (now the Roman Catholic Church) and Eastern, Byzantine Christianity (now the Orthodox Churches), and broken again in the sixteenth century with the split between the Catholic Church and the churches of the Reformation. Many denominations emerged after the Reformation, including the Anglican, Baptist, Lutheran, Methodist, and Presbyterian Churches. Since the middle of the twentieth century, greater unity between Christian communities has been pursued with some success. Some Christians treat the Bible as infallible and inerrant in its original form (free from error), while others treat the Bible as authoritative and inspired but not free from historical error or fallible human influence.

Islam traces its roots back to Judaism and Christianity, acknowledging a common, Abrahamic past. Islamic teaching was forged by the Prophet Mohammed (570–632), who proclaimed a radical monotheism that explicitly repudiated both the polytheism of his time and the Christian understanding of the incarnation and the Trinity. The Qur'an (from *Qu'ra* for 'to recite' or 'to read'), its holy book, was, according to tradition, received by Mohammed, who dictated this revelation of Allah (Arabic for 'God') revealed to him by the Archangel Gabriel, and is taken to be God's very speech. Central to Islam is the sovereignty of Allah, his providential control of the cosmos, the importance of living justly and compassionately, and that of following a set practice of prayer, worship, and pilgrimage.

A follower of Islam is called a Muslim, an Arabic term for 'one who submits', for a Muslim submits to God. The Five Pillars of Islam are reciting the Islamic creed, praying five times a day while facing Mecca, alms–giving, fasting during Ramadan (the ninth month of the Muslim calendar), and making a pilgrimage to Mecca. The two greatest branches of Islam are the Sunnis and Shi'ites, which developed early in the history of Islam over a disagreement about who would succeed Mohammed. Sunnis comprise a vast majority of Muslims. Shi'ites put greater stress on the continuing revelation of God beyond the Qur'an as revealed in the authoritative teachings of the *iman* (holy successors who inherit Mohammed's 'spiritual abilities'), the *mujtahidun* ('doctors of the law'), and other agents.

Like Christianity, Islam has proclaimed that a loving, merciful, and just God will not annihilate an individual at death, but provide either heaven or hell.

Hinduism and Buddhism

While Judaism, Christianity, and Islam originated in the Near East, the other two major world religions, Hinduism and Buddhism, originated in Asia.

Hinduism is so diverse that it is difficult to use the term as an umbrella category even to designate a host of interconnected ideas and traditions. 'Hindu' is Persian for 'Indian' and names the various traditions that have flourished in the Indian subcontinent, going back to before the second millennium BCE. The most common feature of what is considered Hinduism is reverence for the Vedic scriptures, a rich collection of work, some of it highly philosophical, especially the *Upanishads* (written between 800 and 500 BCE). Unlike the three monotheistic religions, Hinduism does not look back to a singular historical figure such as Abraham.

According to one strand of Hinduism, Advaita Vedanta (a strand that has received a great deal of attention from Western philosophers in the twentieth and twenty-first centuries), this world of space and time is ultimately illusory. The world is *Maya* (literally 'illusion'). The world appears to us to consist of diverse objects because we are in a state of ignorance. Behind the diverse objects and forms we observe in what may be called the phenomenal or apparent world (the world of phenomena and appearances) there is the formless, impersonal reality of Brahman, and this school's principal aim is the rejection of this duality ('Advaita' comes from the Sanskrit term for 'nonduality').

Brahman alone is ultimately real. This position is often called *monism* (from the Greek *monus* or 'single') or *pantheism* ('God is everything'). Shankara (also spelled Sankara, Samkara, or Sankaracharya) (788–820) was one of the greatest teachers of this monist, non-dualist tradition within Hinduism. In his *Crest Jewel of Discrimination* he explained that 'Brahman alone is real. There is none but He. When He is known as the supreme reality there is no other existence but Brahman' (Shankara 1970, 82). 'In dream', he wrote in the same book, 'the mind creates by its own power a complete universe of subject and object. The waking state [too] is only a prolonged dream. The phenomenal universe exists in the mind' (71).

Other, theistic strands of Hinduism construe the divine as personal, all-good, powerful, knowing, creative, loving, and so on. Theistic elements may be seen, for example, in the *Bhagavad Gita* (sixth century BCE) and its teaching about the love of God. Some of the breathtaking passages about Krishna's divine manifestation seem similar to the great passages in the Gospel of John when Christ proclaims or implies his divinity or divine calling. Madhva (thirteenth and fourteenth centuries) is one of the better-known theistic representatives of Hinduism.

There are also lively polytheistic elements within Hinduism. Popular Hindu practice includes a rich polytheism, and for this reason it has been called the religion of 330 million gods. The recognition and honor paid to these gods are sometimes absorbed into Brahman worship, since the gods are understood to be so many manifestations of the one true reality.

Whether their beliefs are monist or theistic, many Hindus believe that a trinity of Brahma, Vishnu, and Shiva is the cardinal, supreme manifestation of Brahman. Brahma is the creator of the world, Vishnu its sustainer, manifested in the world as Krishna and Rama, incarnations or avatars (from the Sanskrit for 'one who descends') who instruct and enlighten, and Shiva the destroyer.

Most Hindus believe in reincarnation. The soul migrates through different lives, according to principles of *karma* (Sanskrit for 'deed' or 'action'), the moral consequence of one's actions. The final consummation or enlightenment is *moksha* (or release) from *samsara*, the material cycle of birth and rebirth. In the monist forms, liberation comes from overcoming the dualism of Brahman and the individual self or soul (*atman*, 'breath'), and sometimes from merging into a transcendental self with which all other selves are identical.

Karma is often associated with (and believed to be a chief justification for) a strict social caste system. Not all Hindus support such a system, and many Hindu reformers in the modern era argue for its abolition. One of the well-known reform movements is the Arya Samaj, founded by Swami Dananda Saraswati (1824–83).

Hinduism has a legacy of inclusive spirituality. It understands other religions as different ways to enlightened unity with Brahman. In the *Bhagavad Gita*, Krishna declares,

> If any worshipper do reverence with
> faith to any God whatever,
> I make his faith firm,
> and in that faith he reverences his
> god,
> and gains his desires,
> for it is I who bestow them.

(vii, 21–2)

Hinduism has also absorbed and, to some extent, integrated some of the teaching and narratives of Buddhism. It has also assimilated Christian elements, especially since on the onset of British colonial rule, Jesus being seen as the tenth avatar of Vishnu. Although Hinduism and Islam have sometimes been in painful conflict, there are cases of tolerance and collaboration. One of the aims of Sikhism, a sixteenth-century reform movement within Hinduism, was to bring together Hindus and Muslims.

Buddhism emerged from Hinduism, tracing its origin to Gautama Sakyamuni, who lived in northern India sometime between the sixth and fourth centuries BCE and came to be known as the Buddha ('Enlightened One'). His teaching centers on the Four Noble Truths. These are that: (1) life is full of suffering, pain, and misery (*dukka*); (2) the origin of suffering is in desire (*tanha*); (3) the extinction of suffering can be brought about by the extinction of desire; and (4) the way to extinguish desire is by following the Noble Eightfold Path. The Eightfold Path consists of right understanding; right aspirations or attitudes; right speech; right conduct; right livelihood; right effort; mindfulness; and contemplation or composure.

Early Buddhist teaching tended to be non-theistic, underscoring instead the absence of the self (*anatta*) and the impermanence of life. In its earliest forms, Buddhism did not have a developed metaphysics (that is, a theory of the structure of reality, the nature of space, time, and so on), but did include belief in reincarnation, skepticism about the substantial nature of persons existing over time, and either a denial of the existence of Brahman or the treatment of Brahman as inconsequential. This is its clearest departure from Hinduism. The goal of the religious life is *Nirvana*, a transformation of human consciousness that involves the shedding of the illusion of selfhood.

Schools of Buddhism include Theravada Buddhism, the oldest and strictest in terms of promoting the importance of monastic life, Mahayana, which emerged later and displays less resistance to Hindu themes and does not place as stringent an emphasis on monastic vocation, Pure Land Buddhism, and Zen.

The definition of religion

Many countries have laws about religion. In the United States, these laws prohibit the compulsory imposition of religion, protect religious liberty, and exempt some religious institutions from taxation. A good, common definition of 'religion' is required if these laws are to be well defined. Consensus on a definition would help us decide, for example, whether the theory that God created life on earth is a religious theory that should not be taught in public schools or a scientific theory that can and should be.

In light of the above brief overview of the five world religions, how should one define 'religion'? Unfortunately, religion is not easy to define. Consider six possible definitions.

(1) In *Breaking the Spell* the American philosopher Daniel Dennett defines religions 'as social systems whose participants avow belief in a supernatural agent or agents whose approval is to be sought. This is … a circuitous way of articulating the idea that a religion without God or gods is like a vertebrate without a backbone' (Dennett 2006, 9). This definition will include Abrahamic faiths and some forms of Hinduism. It also rightly sees much of religion in terms of seeking something transcendent that is a vital reference point in terms of value or divine approval.

And yet this definition faces at least two difficulties. First, traditions we recognize as religious, like Therevada Buddhism and forms of Daoism, do not have a God or gods. Second, in some religions God or the divine is conceived of in highly impersonal terms and not as a being who approves or disapproves of human activity. In some forms of Hinduism, for example, Brahman transcends personal manifestations and intentions.

Dennett's definition appears to be too narrow. (A definition is too narrow if it excludes traditions or institutions that we have reason to believe should be considered religious, and it is too broad if it includes traditions or institutions that there is reason to think should not be included.)

(2) Consider the American anthropologist Clifford Geertz's famous definition of religion:

> (1) A system of symbols which acts to (2) establish powerful, pervasive, and long-lasting moods and motivations in men by (3) formulating conceptions of a general order of existence and (4) clothing these conceptions with an aura of factuality that (5) the moods and motivations seem uniquely characteristic.
>
> (Clifford Geertz, cited by Dennett 2006, 391)

This definition seems richer than Dennett's, because it highlights symbols, emotions, and motives. Unfortunately, however, the definitions appears to be too broad. Secular institutions like the National Science Foundation in the United States and totalitarian governments such as Maoist China have routinely advanced systems of symbols, pervasive moods, motivations, and so on, and yet it would be odd to thereby count them as religious. The definition is also needlessly obscure; it seems peculiar to think of Jesus or Buddha promoting a 'mood' rather than a way of life, and the meaning of 'aura of factuality' is hard to pin down. Does the National Science Foundation have a greater aura than, say, the Roman Catholic Church? Perhaps, but how can we form a clear concept of "an aura of factuality?"

Geertz's definition seems both too broad and too obscure or vague.

(3) At one point in *Breaking the Spell*, Dennett seems to allow, in principle, an expanded definition of 'religion', for he takes on

the question of whether his own orientation to science (evolutionary theory, in particular) might constitute a religion. He thinks evolutionary theory provides an awesome, essential means to bring about 'salvation' and is a proper object of 'delight', 'love', and 'glory' and he wishes to 'spread the word' about evolution. (Dennett is a naturalist who might consider himself an apologist.) But then he claims that his view is *not* religious, because religion obstructs clear, rational reflection and promotes incomprehensibility and mystery: '[T]here is a major difference,' he writes.

> We who love evolution do not honor those whose love of evolution prevents them from thinking clearly and rationally about it! ... In our view, there is no safe haven for mystery or incomprehensibility. Yes, there is humility, and awe, and sheer delight, at the glory of the evolutionary landscape, but it is not accompanied by, or in the service of, a willing (let alone thrilling) abandonment of reason. So I feel a moral imperative to spread the word of evolution, but evolution is not my religion. I don't have a religion.
>
> (Dennett 2006, 268)

Regardless of whether you think Dennett does have a religion, his suggestion that religion should be defined as that which is contrary to clear reflection as determined by Daniel Dennett begs the question. All the great world religions, East and West, have advanced philosophies of the sacred which have a serious claim to be considered acts of clear reflection. Moreover, the bare fact that a tradition obstructs reason cannot alone be a reliable sign that it is a religion. Lots of secular political parties and philosophies may obstruct reason without thereby becoming religious.

This definition of Dennett's therefore seems to be question-begging, too broad (it would include institutions that are secular and yet obstruct reason) as well as too narrow (it would exclude religions that promote clear, rational inquiry).

(4) The Canadian philosopher John Schellenberg proposes we define religious propositions or claims as those that assert or entail there is an ultimate reality 'in relation to which an ultimate good can be attained. Otherwise put, religious claims are claims entailing that there is an ultimate and salvific reality' (Schellenberg 2007, 3). This gives center stage to goodness (or what is believed to be good) and to an ultimate or unsurpassable worldview, something all the prominent world religions do. The definition is promising, but there is some reason to think it is too broad. If we adopt Schellenberg's definition, explicit secular views of the world as ultimate and the source of goodness (like Dennett's) would wind up being defined as religious, even though their advocates clearly renounce religion. Like Geertz's definition, Schellenberg's seems too broad.

(5) 'Religion' might also be defined by example: 'Religions include, Judaism, Christianity, Islam, Hinduism, and Buddhism, and those traditions like them.' (Arguably, this is the definition most widely employed by the United States Supreme Court.) There is nothing, in principle, wrong by defining a term by examples ('color' is frequently defined by referring to red, orange, yellow, and so on), and this method has the advantage of leaving open-ended what kinds of things are 'religious'. But I have proposed this view elsewhere and it has been challenged for being too broad: 'Taliaferro's definition may or may not include atheism, Marxism, sport, and nationalism' (Modeé 2005, 21).

By way of a reply, I suggest that American football and soccer in Italy *can* resemble the religions so much that they might well be rightly considered religious. (Traditional religions might view these activities as idolatrous or perversions of a worthy, religious practice of worship.) And political ideologies like Marxism certainly resemble a religion like Christianity.

Marxism has a kind of prophet (Marx himself) and a scripture (his writings) that promotes something like the kingdom of heaven (the rule of the proletariat) through triumphant suffering (class warfare finally transcended by revolution).

But while I persist in thinking this definition acceptable, I recognize the importance of arriving at a more informative definition. Let us then consider one further definition that combines a number of the alternatives.

(6) A religion is a body of teachings and prescribed practices about an ultimate, sacred reality or state of being that calls for reverence or awe and guides its practitioners into what they describe as a saving, illuminating, and emancipatory relationship to this reality through a personally transformative life of prayer, ritualized meditations, and/or moral practices like repentance and moral and personal regeneration.

This definition covers all the major world religions, but I confess it is quite abstract and may still leave us with cases that fit but are not usually thought of as religious. It is more selective than the earlier definitions (Dennett's love of evolution would turn out to be secular, given definition 6, since he does not propose praying to evolution or engaging in ritual meditation), but I leave it to you to improve upon or to replace definition 6 with a better one.

Religions as worlds and worldviews

Enough with definitions! We can overdo linguistic analyses. Having gotten a rough but adequate definition of religion, let us consider what initially seems the natural role of philosophy with respect to religion. I suggest a metaphor for religion that will help us understand this role.

We sometimes refer to 'the art world', 'the world of sports', or 'the world of chess', and I propose that it is natural to think of different religions as different worlds: there is 'the world of Judaism', 'the world of Christianity', 'the world of Buddhism', and so on. The terms are fitting to use of religion because exploring a religion is very much like exploring a world. Just as finding one's way into 'the world of agriculture' involves grasping some biology, ecology, and cultural anthropology, finding one's way into the world of a religion involves grasping its central tenets and beliefs about the sacred. The term also offers a useful way of visualizing the relationship between religions, as circles with some parts overlapping and some separate. The worlds of Judaism, Christianity, and Islam may be seen as overlapping, while each also contains elements not shared by the other two religions.

Additionally, seeing religions as worlds provides a natural way to depict conversions. A convert to a religion may be understood as entering a new world. An analogy may be useful. You cannot see the world of chess if all you see is a colored board with toys placed on squares. To see – let alone enter – the world of chess, you must grasp the rules and know the experience of playing the game. Some seek to enter a new world but do not quite make it. David Hume (1711–76) tells us of a young Turk who was instructed in the Christian religion and 'at last agreed to receive the sacraments of baptism and the Lord's supper', taking the name 'Benedict'.

> The priest, however, to make every thing sure and solid, still continued his instructions, and began the next day with the usual question, How many Gods are there? None at all, replies Benedict; for that was his new name. How! None at all! cries the priest. To be sure, said the honest proselyte. You have told me all along that there is but one God: And yesterday I ate him.
>
> (Hume 1976, 68)

Benedict did not really understand the world of Christianity in which God's sacramental presence in bread and wine is not a literal transformation in which the whole of God becomes no more than a piece of bread that is destroyed when eaten.

Entering the world of a new religion must also involve some affective appreciation of the relevant emotions. You might go to a yoga class, but if you treat it only as a stretching exercise and do not know the role of yoga in the Hindu practice of leading an individual into union with the universal soul (to cite one school of yoga) you have not fully experienced yoga as an affective and spiritual discipline. You have not entered its world. People who identify themselves as Christians and yet hate other people have left the world of Christianity. In my view, the command that Christ's followers love others, including their enemies, is simply too foundational to the religion (e.g. 'If someone says, "I love God," and hates his brother, he is a liar' [I John 4:20]) to be seen as optional. Though I have been describing religions as worlds, one may also refer to 'the secular world' and describe the experience of someone who comes to renounce their religious upbringing as leaving the world of some religion and entering the secular world.

If religions are like worlds, what is the task of philosophy? A natural task, and one that has been undertaken throughout the history of philosophy, is to elucidate a clear account of the beliefs and practices making up such a world and to inquire into reasons for thinking such a world is actually true. It may be that a philosopher concludes (as some have) that there are no compelling intellectual reasons for accepting one or more of the world religions, but that such reasons are not required in order for one to be justified in accepting a given religion. A justified belief can be defined here as one that a person embraces without compromising their intellectual integrity. Some philosophers have defended a concept of *faith* that they believe is a legitimate (in principle) orientation to the religious life. But historically the majority of philosophers who have reflected on religion have devoted themselves to reflection on the reasons that favor or challenge religious beliefs and practices, and even those who defend the concept of faith as free from evidence develop reasoned arguments why such faith is legitimate.

Philosophy of religion, historically and today, includes an examination of the most basic beliefs (or objects of faith) in the great world religions. Of the shared conviction of Judaism, Christianity, and Islam that there is one God, for example, the philosophy of religion asks: What does it mean to say 'there is one God'? And do we have any reason to think that God exists? This question about religion and the general question about whether there is a God – quite apart from any religious context – have exercised philosophers throughout the history of ideas.

Before we advance to explore the coherence and justification of religious beliefs, an important challenge needs to be faced. Could it be that religions are not, fundamentally, about truth or falsehood?

Truth and meaning in religion

Some philosophers have argued that religion is fundamentally about values and illuminating or wise images and metaphors, and not about the truth or falsity of the existence of God or Brahman or karma.

The Anglican philosopher Don Cupitt, for example, once wrote that 'I continue ... to pray to God,' but then went on to say that 'God is the mythical embodiment of all one is concerned with in the spiritual life. He is the religious demand and ideal ... the enshriner of values. He is indeed – but as a myth' (Cupitt 1981, 167). The American philosopher Howard Wettstein has proposed that, just as religious believers use parables to express moral truths, the central beliefs of their religions should be treated as illuminating parables and metaphors for living wisely. Religious practitioners may not believe in the factual truth of their religion's claims about God and providence, but they could instead treat their religious narratives as a matter of profoundly important internal meditation. Wettstein describes such a person:

> She, not unlike one who reads the narrative as an actual account of creation, dwells in the potent imagery … For her, of course, the story is not factually correct. But this is, to her mind, almost not worthy of mention; it is both obvious and completely beside the point, the religious point. The powerful religious resonances and intimation of the story are available to her, as they are to the fundamentalist, as a consequence of dwelling so wholeheartedly in the drama of creation.
>
> (Wettstein 1997, 274)

A Jew or Christian may be deeply religious through a wholehearted focus on biblical narratives while at the same time denying that the God those narratives describe actually exists. One can live fully in the world of the Exodus or the Resurrection without believing in a God who saves those in bondage. One of my professors in graduate school, Gordon Kaufman, developed an elaborate interpretation of symbols which seemed to preserve Christianity while not requiring any belief that there is a God. In Kaufman's theology, 'God' refers to the evolution of human creativity as applied in humane directions (e.g. one serves 'God' by responsibly seeking justice). 'Christ' does not refer to the second member of the Trinity or the world's savior, but refers to the value of self-sacrificing love and living inclusively. Kaufman, Wettstein, and Cupitt each offer an account of the world of Christianity that does not include a commitment to believing there is a creator God, a divine–human liberator in the person of Jesus Christ, and so on.

The Welsh philosopher D.Z. Phillips is more difficult to pin down. He does not explicitly describe himself as an atheist, but he appears to hold that to argue there are grounds to believe or disbelieve that there is a God is a deep grammatical or conceptual confusion and that the current and historical practice of philosophy of religion should be shunned. According to Phillips, philosophers should not try to offer reasons for or against the belief in God or Brahman, the afterlife, salvation, or enlightenment, and so on. Phillips's reason for this conclusion is that religious terms like 'God' and 'Brahman' get their meaning principally and foundationally in religious practices. To refer to 'God' outside of the religious practices that give meaning to the term is to misunderstand the term 'God'. Phillips thinks it proper (involving no distinctively philosophical error) to pray to God or sing hymns or seek to live life before God, but he thinks that once a philosopher seeks to ask whether God exists and to come up with reasons for or against God's existence, that philosopher has ceased to make sense.

These four proposals to remove religion from philosophical scrutiny are significant, but I suggest that they do not give us reason to reject the ancient and still widespread practice of philosophically exploring and arguing about religious beliefs about reality. Cupitt, Wettstein, and Kaufman are straightforward in their rejection of theism (though Wettstein has changed his mind subsequently). If atheism is in fact true, those of us who pray to God are only praying to an image of a being that does not exist, and our love for God is not the love of an actual being, but more like the love of a fictional character. As H.D. Lewis argues in *Our Experience of God*, religious practices like prayer are profoundly different from the practice of meditating on what is known to be fictitious.

> We take delight in fiction as well as in fact, and the extent to which spice is added to a story by knowing that it is true must,

I imagine, vary a great deal from one individual to another ... But whether or not the value of fiction turns on some subtle truth it succeeds in conveying, it is certain that religion would [have] lost its hold upon us if we had to regard it as fiction. If someone invented a religion, however colorful its rites and attractive the ideas to be entertained within it, we could not take it seriously unless we were convinced of its truth. We cannot just divert ourselves with a religion or play at it.

(Lewis 1959, 21)

If Lewis is right, religious practice is inextricably bound up with the conviction that these practices truly reflect reality. It may be that Kaufman, Wettstein, and Cupitt can redefine religious terms so that when someone claims to believe in God they are only asserting that it is good to pursue goodness creatively, but it is hard to believe that, historically and today, this is a reasonable account of what most people mean when they claim to believe in or love God.

As for Phillips, though there is not space to examine his views in detail, on close consideration, the arguments he advances for his claim that we should not philosophically debate whether God exists turn out to be arguments that God (as understood in theism) does not exist. So Phillips has argued extensively that though prayer has a good role in religious life, once you ask whether there is a divine personal or person-like reality that actually hears the prayers and responds to petitions or prayers for forgiveness, you have made a mistake. That's because such a being would have to be imagined to hear without sense organs, for God (as traditionally conceived) is incorporeal and without ears. Phillips writes that to argue about whether 'you can hear without ears, or see without eyes, is a good example of language going on a holiday', by which he means that it is an example of failing to understand terms like 'prayer'. So Phillips adopts the paradoxical position of claiming that it is nonsense to think there is a God who actually hears prayers, but at the same time he does not want to deny that (in a religious ritual of praying) God hears prayers.

> The consequence, however, is not to deny the sense of saying that we live under God's eye, or that he hears our prayers, or to start speculating about the superiority of divine listening and seeing equipment. Instead, we should look for the meaning of these expressions in religious practice.

> (Phillips 2007, 301)

Phillips rightly draws attention to the ways in which the terminology of 'God' and 'prayer' is anchored in religious practices, but it is very difficult to believe that most religious persons would continue praying if they were convinced there is no divine reality listening. It certainly appears that when persons in the monotheistic religions pray to God they are addressing what they believe to be a merciful, supreme creator who lovingly hears and cares for their petition and has the power to respond. If *everyone* became convinced that there is no such being, why would *anyone* continue to petition, praise, or confess to the divine? It seems that religious believers and skeptics alike have a stake in exploring the reasons for and against the reality of a divine being who may be encountered through prayer, meditation, and experience.

While I propose that philosophy has a proper role in developing reasons for and against religious belief, I suggest that the challenge by Phillips and the others should lead us to appreciate that if we are engaged in philosophy of *religion*, and not just the philosophy of *God*, we should not neglect actual religious beliefs and practices. This is something I stress in later chapters. Also, if it turns out we may reasonably conclude that the foundational beliefs of a religion are false, it could still be the case that the religion has produced profoundly important insights. If there is no God, maybe Cupitt or Wettstein or Kaufman is right that we should still live as though there is a God of love or we should retain religious language in order to express our deep commitment to the creative pursuit of justice. Even if one concludes that atheism is right and the monotheistic religions mistaken, there is still the possibility that these religions have vital moral content and meaning that should still be taken seriously.

In the next chapter, let us consider some concepts of God and divine attributes, and then, in chapter 3, some of the classical and contemporary arguments for and against the existence of God.

2
Concepts of God

In this chapter let us consider the concept of God that is foundational for the Abrahamic faiths. A great deal of work in the philosophy of religion is focused on elucidating the concept of God and its coherence. The importance of this task is difficult to overestimate, since without a clear, coherent understanding of the meaning of the concept of God, arguments about whether or not God exists become profoundly confused and unhelpful.

The literature in the past and today on the coherence of theism is vast, for philosophers and theologians have raised serious arguments about the extent to which we can form an intelligible concept of God using human language. At some points, there has been a peculiar similarity between atheists and mystics: atheists arguing that there cannot be a God because the very concept of God is incoherent, and mystics arguing that there are compelling religious grounds for seeking God beyond our best language and symbols. As we make our way into the world of theism, it is good to contemplate the African philosophical theologian St Augustine's (354–430) famous lines in which he acknowledges both the difficulty and importance of using language about God:

> You, my God, are supreme, utmost in goodness, mightiest and all-powerful, most merciful and most just. You are the most hidden from us and yet the most present amongst us, the most beautiful and yet the most strong, ever enduring and yet we cannot comprehend you … Can any man say enough when he speaks of you? Yet woe betide those who are silent about you!

> For even those who are most gifted with speech cannot find
> words to describe you.
>
> (1991 [430], I, 4)

Traditionally, theists have sought to balance positive claims about God (technically referred to as *cataphatic theology*) with an acknowledgement of the importance of negative claims (*apophatic theology*). What follows involves positive claims in theistic world religion, but at the end of the chapter we will consider the limits of language.

God as maximally excellent

In the worlds of Judaism, Christianity, and Islam, the divine is a reality of unsurpassable greatness, with unrivaled sovereignty as creator and as a moral compass for human life, worthy of our highest allegiance, awe, loyalty, and worship. The goodness of human and all life and the good of the whole creation is believed to be derived from the goodness of God. The Psalms (authoritative for Judaism and Christianity) proclaim God's great goodness (e.g. Psalms 31:19, 106:1) and describe God's work and being as perfect (Psalm 19:7; see also Matthew 5:48), for example, while the Qur'an depicts God as mighty wisdom and truth, deserving all praise (Sura 31).

Philosophers have worked hard to refine the concept of God as unsurpassably good and worthy of praise, by developing the attributes that make God God: God's necessary or underived existence, incorporeality, omnipotence, essential goodness, omniscience, omnipresence, and eternity. Each divine attribute enhances the others. For example, a being that was omnipotent but not omniscient would appear to be less excellent than a being both omnipotent and omniscient.

Let us consider some of the divine attributes alone and in relationship to each other.

Necessary or non-contingent existence

A state of affairs is contingent if it is possible that it will occur and also possible that it will not. So, the state of affairs of *there being horses* is contingent because we could have lived in a universe without horses. Philosophers in the Islamic tradition have been especially committed to articulating the thesis that God's existence is not contingent. One way they (and later Jewish and Christian thinkers) expressed the concept is by claiming that God's very essence (what it is to be God) contains existence. With respect to everything else in this world, its essence (*what it is*) is distinct from *its existence (the fact of its existing or not existing)*. At one time horses did not exist and it is likely that one day horses will cease to exist. (Astrophysicists conjecture that when the sun uses all its helium, in four billion years, the earth will vaporize.) The concept of God, however, unlike horses, planets, and suns, is not contingent, because (if there is a God) God never came into existence nor can God cease to be. God's very essence is existence. To be God is to exist. Because God's very essence is existence, to ask why God exists (or 'who created God') would be like asking 'Is red red?' Red *is* red, by definition and the law of identity (A is A, or everything is itself). Similarly, the very concept of God is the concept of a reality that (if God exists) God could not have been created by any other reality. Traditional theists sometimes express this point by saying that God possesses *aseity* (self-existence); God exists *a se* (Latin for 'being for oneself') as opposed to *ab alio* (being from another) or having a conferred or derived existence. We shall return to this in considering the ontological argument for God's existence, in the next chapter.

Incorporeality

God is sometimes portrayed in the scriptures of the monotheistic traditions in terms of a material embodiment: Adam and Eve 'heard the sound of the Lord God walking in the garden' (Genesis 1:8). But virtually all philosophical theists interpret these passages as metaphors to describe God, who is a non-physical reality: a being not identical with any material object. 'God is spirit' (John 4:24). To describe God as walking in the Garden of Eden is a vivid way of describing the felt proximity of God. Traditional Christians believe God became incarnate (embodied), but this is not the same thing as believing God has turned into a corporeal object.

Consider this objection: Some philosophers have argued that there might be a very powerful, knowledgeable, good God only if this being had a body like Zeus or Thor, because an incorporeal agent is a contradiction of terms. Don't all coherent ideas about agents or persons require being embodied?

The difficulty with this objection is that there does not appear to be anything about being an agent or person (a subject who intentionally brings about events) that ipso facto requires any kind of body. Agents are not *necessarily* physical or embodied. Even if we humans are essentially embodied (viz. we cannot exist without our bodies), it does not follow that *every* conceivable (or unconceivable) being is corporeal.

Besides, even in our own case, it is difficult to establish that our power of agency (our desire and ability to bring about some event) is itself purely physical. We can observe what happens in the brain when a person desires to think about mathematics, but arguably that is not to observe the person's desire to think about mathematics. Contemporary brain science has not shown how our subjective experience (our thinking, sensing, and emotions) can be the very same thing as our brain processes. If all we knew about a person was limited to purely physical processes (an exhaustive study of anatomy in physics and chemistry) we would not thereby be aware of the person's psychological or mental states. There is good evidence of correlation between the psychological and the physical; damage to the brain causes psychological harm or even the irretrievable loss of consciousness. But causal correlation and dependency is not the same thing as identity. (Actually, the *correlation* of the psychological and bodily processes implies non-identity; in medicine we correlate mental states with physical states as opposed to discovering that the two are identical.) And even if it turns out that our mental states and activities are the very same things as our brain activity, this discovery of something true about ourselves does not require us to rule out the possibility of other agents being incorporeal agents. (Chapter 5 includes further arguments about human nature and the physical world.)

Divine incorporeality is closely related to divine necessary existence, for it has appeared to many philosophers that physical, corporeal objects are contingent. It is also related to the belief that God is omnipresent or everywhere. If God were some giant or tiny corporeal object, it would be difficult to think of God as everywhere.

Omnipotence

The idea that God is all-powerful is a very early, foundational principle of monotheism. Part of what distinguished monotheistic religious traditions is their creation stories. Unlike many of the stories of the gods of Mesopotamia and the Greco-Roman world, in which creation involved procreation or sometimes violence, even disembowelment, the God of monotheism creates with unrivaled power. In Genesis, creation is portrayed in terms of divine commands in the form of speech. The use of speech is an example of a metaphorical or symbolic reference to God, expressing God's primary or central reality as *purposive*. In theism, God is not an impersonal force or event; creation is described with terms that refer to a key way in which purpose and intelligence are manifested (language) as opposed to mindless processes or events (like an accidental noise or explosion). The use of speech as a metaphor in Genesis also conveys to Jews and Christians that God is a God of communication and revelation. If God can speak, perhaps humans should listen for God.

Puzzles arise with respect to omnipotence, however, in two ways: internally and externally. Internal puzzles concern only the attribute itself, whereas external puzzles emerge when the attribute is paired with other divine attributes.

The most famous of the internal difficulties is framed in terms of a task that an omnipotent being cannot perform. Here is one version, sometimes called 'The Paradox of the Stone'. These puzzles date back to the fourteenth century, perhaps earlier.

1. An omnipotent being is a being able to do any act.
2. If God is omnipotent, God can create a stone so heavy that no one can lift.
3. If God is omnipotent, God can lift any stone.
4. But if God can lift any stone, then God cannot create a stone so heavy that no one can lift it.
5. And if God can create a stone so heavy that no one can lift it, then there could be a stone that not even God could lift.
6. There is at least one act God cannot do.
7. Hence, God is not omnipotent. (Some will argue – more radically – that, since God must be omnipotent to be God, this proves that God does not exist.)

The most common way to address this puzzle is by refining premise 1 to: 'An omnipotent being is a being able to do any *possible* act.' There cannot be a stone so heavy that a being who can lift any stone cannot lift it. It only appears possible if we are actually picturing a less powerful being than God. You and I can build objects so heavy that we cannot lift them, but a being that can do anything possible cannot (for logical reasons) create an object that such a being cannot lift.

I think this is a decisive reply to 'The Paradox of the Stone'. There is no need to undertake philosophical acrobatics, as some philosophers do, by arguing that God can do what is logically incoherent or could choose to limit God's powers (create a stone and choose to be unable to lift it).

Part of the problem with this argument is that by insisting that omnipotence should include the ability to do the logically impossible it removes our ability to think about these matters altogether. Strictly speaking, we cannot imagine that which is logically impossible; no one can picture a round square, an object that both has and does not have four right angles.

A more vexing problem with omnipotence arises when the attribute is paired with other divine properties, especially *essential goodness*, which I think is no mere add-on in theistic religious tradition. Let us consider this problem next.

Essential goodness

Some passages in the scriptures of the monotheistic traditions imply that God can do no evil, e.g. 'It is impossible for God to lie' (Hebrews 6:18). The idea that God is essentially good follows from the idea that God is maximally excellent. If that is right, then it appears that a being cannot be both omnipotent and essentially good. Arguably, being capable of falling into evil and wickedness is not excellent.

Some theists do not accept the notion that God is essentially good, offering against it 'the argument from praise'.

1. An agent does a praiseworthy act when the agent does the act, but could have done otherwise.
2. If God is essentially good, then God cannot be praised for doing only good acts, for God could not do otherwise.
3. Therefore, either God is not praiseworthy or not essentially good.

One reply to this is that although God's essential goodness entails that 'God does no evil' or, even more strongly, 'God can do no evil', it does not fix *all* divine action. That is, while creating a cosmos may be good, God does not have to do it. If God did not create the cosmos, no thing or person would have been harmed. The creation itself is commonly regarded in theistic tradition as a gift and the divine giver may rightly be praised for giving such a gift that was not merited or required. It should also be pointed out, against premise 1, that the praise directed toward God in theistic religions is not clearly a form of *moral praise*, as when you praise someone for good behavior. The praise of God is more akin to the awe and reverence one feels in the face of something sublime. When one feels awe in response to a breathtaking mountain range or an overwhelming humility and delight in response to Hubble spacecraft pictures of planets and galaxies, or in response to childbirth, this awe or delight is not a moral matter, but something more encompassing.

But even if we reject the argument from praise, the idea that God is both omnipotent and essentially good does give rise to the following difficulty.

1. An omnipotent being is able to do any logically possible act.
2. An essentially good being is not able to do evil.
3. Doing evil is a logically possible act.
4. Because God is essentially good, God cannot do any logically possible act.
5. Therefore, God is not omnipotent.

The argument might be re-formulated by comparing God with a God-like being that is not essentially good, whom we may call Molich.

1. If God is essentially good, then God is not able to do evil.
2. There cannot be a being more powerful than God.
3. There could be a being, Molich, with all God's properties except essential goodness.

4. If Molich exists, Molich can do any act God can do, plus any evil act.
5. In this case, Molich would be more powerful than God.
6. Conclusion: God is not essentially good or God is not unsurpassable in power or – more radically – there is no God.

Various logical maneuvers have been used in replying to these arguments. For example, it has been argued that an essentially good being can do evil to accomplish a greater good. But this strategy is only partly successful; presumably, great goods would only allow for some divine acts. Molich could torture people for the sake of entertainment, but an essentially good God cannot. It has also been replied that God, although essentially good, has the *ability to do evil* but *cannot do evil*. (Imagine someone like Mother Theresa: she has the power to push an innocent person under a bus, but, given her character, she cannot do so.) Perhaps that reply is sufficient.

I suggest the more promising reply to these difficulties is to contend that the ability to do evil is not a power that is proper to a maximally excellent being, as has been argued by Augustine, Boetheus (480–526), and Aquinas (1224/5–75). For free human creatures, our ability to do wrong might be an essential reflection (or the necessary complement) of our ability to freely do good, but for a God with unsurpassable excellence the ability to do evil is a liability – a condition of vulnerability to corruption and degradation. The power of God is best thought of in terms not of bare power but of perfect, praiseworthy power.

This stress on *perfect* power in a philosophy of God is in keeping with feminist objections to the concept of God as sheer power. The early modern feminist Mary Wollstonecraft (1759–97) complained that men tend to privilege brute power in their concept of God:

> Man, accustomed to bow down to power in his savage state, can seldom divest himself of this barbarous prejudice, even when civilization determines how much superior mental is to bodily strength; and his reason is clouded by these crude opinions, even when he thinks of the Deity. – His omnipotence is made to swallow up, or preside over his other attributes, and those mortals are supposed to limit his power irreverently, who think that it must be regulated by his wisdom.
>
> (Wollstonecraft 1996, 45)

Wollstonecraft counseled, instead, giving primacy to the goodness of God. More recently, the German Dorothee Soelle has written,

> As a woman I have to ask why it is that human beings honor a God whose most important attribute is power, whose prime need is to subjugate, whose greatest fear is equality … Why should we honor and love a being that does not transcend but only reaffirms the moral level of our present male dominated culture? Why should we honor and love this being … if his being is in fact no more than an outsized man?
>
> (Soelle 1984, 97)

These feminist concerns bring to light the ways in which concepts of God are often interwoven with cultural history. During periods when monarchs or state bodies have emphasized absolute power, there has been a tendency to view God as more like Molich. In contrast, social reformers in religious cultures have tended to recognize the primacy of *goodness* (or *perfect power*) (see Taliaferro and Tepley 2005).

Omniscience

The thesis that God is all-knowing has generated substantial philosophical attention, especially concerning the scope of divine knowledge. The chief focus has been on 'future free contingents', future events that are genuinely contingent, not predetermined, such as those which involve the exercise of free choice. On one plausible libertarian view of freedom, freedom involves the possibility of doing something while possessing the ability to do otherwise. But what if God knows perfectly and precisely that you will give to Oxfam tomorrow? If so, the future seems fixed. If God knows what you will do tomorrow, you cannot do otherwise. But if the future is fixed, how can you be free? This argument has not been an idle one historically. The reformer Martin Luther (1483–1546) used the appeal to divine omniscience to deny we possess radical freedom. He insisted instead on a stringent idea of God's providential Lordship over the future. Luther opposed what he saw as the vanity of human beings in refusing to acknowledge our absolute dependence upon God's grace.

There are several additional replies.

The first is simply to claim that the objection falsely assumes that divine knowledge that you will freely give to Oxfam tomorrow undermines your freedom. If you freely will do X tomorrow and have the power to do otherwise, the foreknowledge of what you will freely do does not at all imply that you couldn't do otherwise. To adopt an analogy from ancient Greek philosophy, if you foreknow what chariot will win the race tomorrow, your foreknowledge does not determine the winner. An objector might protest that you could know the victor only if the race were fixed, but two points can be made against this objection when applied to God: first, God's mode of knowing may be profoundly different from human foreknowledge and, second, since our knowledge of past free action does not in any way undermine an actor's freedom, why should knowledge of the future? Arguably, the paradox about foreknowledge gains intuitive force if we imagine human subjects, in time, knowing in advance what a free agent will do. But if God is not temporal or in time, the paradox may lose its grip on us. See 'Eternity' below.

The second reply invokes a radically comprehensive portrait of divine knowledge. According to some philosophers, God possesses what is called 'middle knowledge', knowing what all possible creatures would do under any condition. Knowing what circumstances you are in at any point in your life, God knows how you will exercise your agency and your power to do otherwise. This exalted understanding of divine knowledge was formulated by the sixteenth-century philosopher Luis de Molina and is defended today by Thomas Flint and William Craig, among others. This is a radical but philosophically interesting option. It is, however, challenged by a third reply.

This third, quite different, reply is worthy of attention: omniscience does not cover future free contingents. If you have not yet given to Oxfam, whether you will or will not do so is not fixed or determined. The truth of statements like 'you will freely give to Oxfam in August 2012' is undetermined and so the statement is neither true nor false now (2009). Because 'omniscience' only covers what can be known to be true or false, future free contingents are not in the domain of omniscience. This option is often associated today with a position called *open theism*. According to open theism, the future for both the creator and creature is genuinely open and not fixed.

Open theists sometimes support their position in reference to the problem of evil. They argue that it is more in keeping with the goodness of God that God created a cosmos with genuine risks rather than creating the cosmos with the future fully determined and foreknown. Some Christians object that the God of open theism is not a God who can guarantee prophecies about the future. Open theists counter that, scripturally, prophecies may be seen as conditional intentions of God. The fulfillment of prophecies involves both God and genuinely free human responses.

Finally, we should consider a relatively recent objection to divine omniscience. A formal version of the argument involves what is called *concept empiricism*.

1. According to concept empiricism, to grasp the concept of a sensation or emotion, a being must have experienced it. To properly grasp the concept *red*, for example, you need to have experienced the color red; to grasp vulnerability you must have been vulnerable; to grasp sadism you must have felt sadistic.
2. Thesis: God is omniscient. God, for example, knows the concepts red, vulnerability, and sadism.
3. Thesis: God is also omnipotent, incorporeal, and essentially good.
4. If premise 1 is true, premises 2 and 3 cannot both be true. If God is incorporeal, God has no sensory cognitive faculties and so cannot experience *red*. If God is omnipotent and thus possesses perfect power, God cannot experience vulnerability. If God is essentially good, God cannot experience sadistic emotions. If God cannot experience such sensations and emotions, God cannot know them and thus God cannot be omniscient.

This is a very interesting argument indeed. The first premise is intuitively plausible. After all, if you knew everything about the concept of *red* (the retinal and brain conditions essential to seeing red, the relevant wavelengths, and so on), but had no sensation of seeing red, it seems that you would not know what red looks like.

But the conclusion can be challenged, by questioning its understanding of the relation of the divine attributes to the emotions and sensations. Many theists claim that an all-powerful God who creates genuinely free creatures might have to limit divine power in order for them to be genuinely free, and thus would experience a kind of self-imposed restraint or weakness. If creatures can genuinely and freely resist God's love, wouldn't a loving God experience vulnerability? In this case, a being could be both omnipotent and know vulnerability simultaneously.

Consider essential goodness and sadism (or any other emotion that is wrong or unjust). The objection that God cannot experience an emotion that is unjust or wicked ignores the possibility that such bad emotions are complex states made up of morally acceptable components wrongly combined or wrongly directed. Arguably, a morally perfect being who hates no one can grasp what it is like to hate persons by grasping the concepts of persons and hate (there is nothing wrong with hatred per se, as in the case of hatred of evil). A good God could grasp the concept of sadism by grasping such concepts as pleasure, pain, subordination, and power.

The argument from concept empiricism may support a deeply censorious view of art. Some works of art have been criticized because they invite readers to adopt the viewpoint of wicked agents. For example, Margaret Atwood's novel *The Blind Assassin* provokes readers to see cruel acts from the point of view of the one inflicting harm. But if considering such a viewpoint automatically makes one cruel or complicit in cruelty, perhaps Atwood, Shakespeare, and C.S. Lewis – the author of *The Screwtape Letters*, which is composed from the standpoint of a demon – should all be censured. If this is the wrong conclusion to reach when it comes to art, isn't there something wrong in claiming that if God knows the points of view of the wicked then God is wicked or imperfect?

One may also question the assumption that God could have no sensations. There is no proof I know of that an incorporeal agent cannot experience sensations. A number of philosophers today (but not a majority) think that sensations are mental properties and not identical with the products of the senses (of the retina, for example) or brain states, though they are caused by both. If this is possible, the argument fails because God could (in theory) experience sensations.

But apart from these ways of replying to the argument from concept empiricism, one may well challenge the first premise (that a being must have an experience of x to understand x).

Even if human creatures cannot grasp x without experiencing x, is this a self-evident principle that governs all possible forms of knowing? Presumably one does not always need to be in a state of x to know x: I do not need to be a square to know about squares, or hot to know that something is hot, or hateful to know that someone is hateful, and so on. Concept empiricism seems built on a premise that knowing something involves a kind of melding in which the x that is known is somehow made integral to the knowing subject, as though x comes to define or mark the knower. Something like this was proposed by David Hume, who held that ideas of sensations were faint or faded sensations. But there seems to be little reason to accept this. My idea about, say, economic recession is not a faded sensation of any kind. There are limits about what we humans can visualize. We can't form a visual image of an object with a thousand sides, but we can conceive of such an object and reflect on its properties.

There are dozens more arguments of this nature on omniscience in the literature today.

Eternity

The idea that God transcends, or is beyond, temporal change has a rich history. To some extent, the great monotheistic traditions inherited a Platonic concept of reality and value, according to which that which is most real and valuable (for Plato, this was described as 'the good') is incorruptible and not subject to the alteration, fragmentation, and decay that comes about through time. Some philosophers have held that God must be eternal because otherwise God is in some way a prisoner of time and unable to enjoy the unity of life that should mark supreme perfection.

A contemporary advocate of God's eternity, Brian Leftow, makes the case this way: the life of a temporal being has what he calls 'inner limits', in which the parts of the being's life are separate from others. Such limitations have their advantages for beings living in time (I am relieved to have finished my doctoral dissertation), but with God these limitations would mark a fragmentation that does not befit the fullness and perfection of the divine nature. A perfect being would have its full being or reality in a complete state, rather than spread out in a past that is gone and in a future that has yet to arrive. On this view, open theism leaves us with an incomplete or imperfect understanding of God's nature.

The thesis that God is eternal may appear at odds with scriptural narratives in which God first does one act and then another. Most theologians in the three monotheistic traditions treat such references to God as highly analogical or metaphorical, because the Hebrew and Christian Bibles and the Qur'an describe God from *our point of view*. We cannot help thinking of God as acting successively in time (first doing one thing, then another), and yet God does not in fact act this way. Some explain this by arguing that God eternally wills succession, that God wills that there will be changes but God's will itself does not change. God's inner being is therefore changeless, not subject to alteration, fragmentation, and decay. God may have a temporal dimension by being 'at' all times or (as Christians believe) in the incarnation, as Jesus Christ in first-century Palestine, but God's inner being is transcendent. God's life is *tota simul*, or all at once, as Boethius famously described it.

This understanding of God has at least two benefits, from a theistic point of view. The belief that God transcends time provides a promising way to address the problem of freedom and foreknowledge discussed earlier. If God is in some sense beyond time, what is for us past and future may be present to God. God therefore does not so much as *foreknow* future acts as grasp them in a divine present moment.

God's transcendence of time has the additional benefit of allowing that God created time. If God is temporally extended (meaning that God has a past, present, and future), God cannot be independent of time and therefore cannot be the creator of time.

There is an enormous literature arguing over whether God is temporally eternal or temporal but without beginning. Consider just one objection and reply.

According to what may be called the *objection from simultaneity*, the relation of simultaneity is transitive. A transitive relationship is one that transfers sequentially: if you are taller than Pat, and Pat is taller than Chris, then you are taller than Chris. Simultaneity appears to be transitive. If I am writing at the same time as you are running, and you are running at the same time Chris is singing, then I am writing at the same time Chris is singing. If God exists simultaneously with Nero burning Rome and with your whistling, then Nero is burning Rome at the same time you are whistling (Kenny 1979, 38–9). Because of the absurdity of the conclusion, some philosophers conclude that God is not eternal.

Defenders of God's eternity have replied that the objection from simultaneity fails, because simultaneity is transitive for temporal creatures like us, but for God all times are present. The life of God is not, as it were, lived instant by instant, but occupies an extended, timeless present. As Leftow puts it, 'An eternal God is God present with the whole of time by His life's being stretched out alongside it' (1991, 117). We can thereby set the objection from simultaneity to one side.

The God of Philosophy and the God of Revelation

Before turning in the next chapter to the main arguments for and against the existence of God, let us briefly consider the possible tension between a philosophy of God grounded principally on the idea of God as a maximally excellent reality and one grounded exclusively on religious texts like the Bible and the Qur'an.

The philosophy of divine attributes described above is certainly related to the theistic scriptures; the Bible and Qur'an portray God as unsurpassably good and worthy of praise. The idea that God is a being principally worthy of praise is secured in the opening of the Qur'an (1:1–7):

> In the name of Allah, Most Gracious, Most Merciful.
> Praise be to Allah, the Cherisher and Sustainer of the worlds;
> Most Gracious, Most Merciful;
> Master of the Day of Judgement.
> Thee do we worship, and Thine aid we seek.
> Show us the straight way,
> The way of those on whom Thou has bestowed Thy Grace,
> those
> whose portion is not wrath, and who go not astray.

The Hebrew and Christian Bibles begin with a creation narrative that is essentially praise of God as creator. And the backbone of Hebrew and Christian spirituality over the centuries has been the recitation of the Psalms with their praise of God as worthy of *unending* praise, whatever human beings face. Muslim, Jewish, and Christian scriptures treat as idolatrous the worship of beings other than God.

Even so, a philosophy of God that stresses God's perfection (sometimes called *perfect being theology*) has been challenged on two fronts: by biblically oriented thinkers who see God as good, rather than perfect or maximally excellent, and by atheists like Dawkins who are convinced that the God of scriptures is (to use the terms once used to describe the romantic poet Byron) mad, bad, and dangerous to know.

Here is Dawkins's evaluation of the scriptural God:

> The God of the Old Testament is arguably the most unpleasant character in all fiction; jealous and proud of it; a petty, unjust, unforgiving control-freak; a vindictive, bloodthirsty ethnic cleanser; a misogynistic, homophobic, racist, infanticidal, genocidal, filicidal, pestilential, megalomaniacal, sadomasochistic, capriciously malevolent bully. Those of us schooled from infancy in his ways can become desensitized to their horror …
> The oldest of the three Abrahamic religions, and the clear ancestor of the other two, is Judaism: originally a tribal cult of a single fiercely unpleasant God, morbidly obsessed with sexual restrictions, with the smell of charred flesh, with his own superiority over rival gods and with the exclusiveness of his chosen desert tribe.
>
> (Dawkins 2006, 31, 37)

It is not possible to address at length both Christians who in the name of the Bible resist seeing God as maximally excellent and Dawkins and others who are contemptuous of the perceived vices of the God of the Bible. I shall resort to a brief reply to both, sketching a line of reasoning for elaboration elsewhere.

A modest reply to those favoring the biblical God to God as perfect being

Almost from the beginning of recorded theological reflection on scripture, Jewish, Christian, and Islamic thinkers interpreted their scriptures in the service of forming a comprehensive understanding of God. If scripture definitively portrays God as loving and just, then either biblical narratives in which God appears neither loving nor just must be interpreted as reflecting fallible human lovelessness and injustice, or theologians need to show how the biblical God is nevertheless consistently loving and just.

Those adopting the first approach invoke the concept of *progressive revelation*. God has been increasingly revealed over time. Precepts in Hebrew scripture that allow slavery are judged to be primitive, merely human projections that eventually give way to the purity and nobility of ethical monotheism as evidenced in the great prophets Isaiah, Jeremiah, Amos, and others. More traditional defenders of the Bible will also allow for progress in revelation while maintaining belief in God's perfection. Any allowance for slavery in the past was a practical accommodation to and limitation of an almost universal practice to be rejected as soon as possible.

There is credibility in both replies, but take note of a way in which the biblical portrait of God may fruitfully modify the perfect being philosophy of God. Monotheistic religions portray God as loving, merciful, and compassionate. Their scriptures speak of God delighting in goodness and sorrowing over injustice. This language suggests God has passion. Perfect being theology has often denied that God has passion and insisted that God is *impassable* (literally, without passion). One argument made for this is that if God is eternal, God does not change (God is *immutable*), and passion involves change. Another argument is that, since God is *active* and not subject to the creation, God cannot be affected by it in the way that creates passions.

But more recent philosophical developments have challenged the idea of divine impassability, arguing that passion might be eternal or that God might be temporal and rightly thought of as undergoing different temporal states. Others ask why suffering love has to be seen as a passive state of being subject to creation. Perhaps love (whether it is sorrowing or joyful) can be understood as supreme action, perhaps even a reflection of a supreme, great-making excellence. (New work in moral psychology by Robert Solomon and others has led many to see the emotions as activities rather than passive states.) This new discussion opens opportunities for the biblical portrait of God to inform perfect being philosophy, bringing a more affective dimension to the philosophy of God.

Reply to the critique of the biblical God with a little help from perfect being philosophy

If biblical sources can enrich perfect being theology, perfect being theology may help defend the biblical God from criticisms like Dawkins's. Let us consider two of his objections as representative of all of them: God is vain and God is jealous. Vanity and jealousy are vices and such a God need not be worshipped or followed.

To all appearances, Dawkins has a good point. The supposed vanity of God can be seen in God's demand to be worshipped and in images of God (isn't that what the biblical God does in creating humans in God's likeness?) The jealousy of God can be seen in the Hebrew Bible and Christian Old Testament's unequivocal 'I, the Lord your God, am a jealous God' (Exodus 20:5).

One way to answer Dawkins's charge is to articulate a philosophy of God as maximally excellent in terms of essential goodness. Given such an understanding of God, the worship of God may be seen as the creature's natural and proper delight in and awe before God's superabundant essential goodness. Because worship of God involves taking delight in goodness itself, worship may be seen as helping to orient creatures toward a good life. The action of this essentially good God in demanding worship can be seen as a reflection of God's great goodness rather than of God's huge ego.

The Hebrew and Christian scriptures often speak of God as a jealous God. Again, Dawkins seems to have a good point, but yet again perfect being theology offers an answer. Is jealousy always a vice? It is a vice when it stems from a presumptuous claim to something to which one has no right. But in a proper or healthy relationship – like that of a parent and child or husband and wife – concerned sorrow or displeasure when the other partner recklessly endangers the relationship is natural and appropriate. Imagine a child who rejects his or her true, caring parents and treats a sexist, racist, drug-addicted, violent philosophy professor as a parent. The parents may rightfully feel a healthy jealousy for their child's love, hoping she or he will return to them. If the biblical portrait defines God, as perfect being theology does, as including essential, perfect goodness, then divine jealousy may be understood as a manifestation of God's desire that the creation be oriented to goodness itself. What is described in biblical terms as jealousy is (like vanity) a statement not about a God with an ego to be satisfied, but about a God who wants human beings to have a life of fitting and fulfilling relationship with God.

I believe that significant progress can be made in assessing Dawkins's objections to theism when one appreciates that Dawkins stipulates that the very concept of God does *not* include goodness. So, in *The God Delusion*, Dawkins defines what he calls 'the God Hypothesis' as the thesis that 'there exists a super-human, supernatural intelligence who deliberately designed and created the universe and everything in it, including us … Goodness is no part of the definition of the God Hypothesis, merely a desirable add on' (Dawkins 2006, 31, 108). But for the Abrahamic faiths goodness is absolutely foundational. Many traditional theists would actually (like Dawkins) reject the 'God Hypothesis' if goodness were a mere 'add-on'. But once one appreciates how the concepts of God and goodness are inter-twined in the worlds of Judaism, Christianity, and Islam one may see some ways to reply to the charges that a jealous God or one that demands worship is vain or wicked.

Many more issues would need to be considered to reply to Dawkins fully, but I hope this outline of a reply might at least stimulate further reflection.

A God beyond language?

Having canvassed the divine attributes in the Abrahamic faiths, let us step back to consider whether there is a profound religious obstacle to this whole enterprise. Theistic scriptures sometimes insist that God is beyond all human thought and language

> For my thoughts are not your thoughts.
> Nor are your ways my ways, says the LORD
> For as the heavens are higher than the earth,
> So are my ways higher than your ways
> And my thoughts than your thoughts.
>
> (Isaiah 55:8–9 [New Revised Standard Version – NRSV])

Earlier in this chapter we noted the tension between the cataphatic and apophatic. Why not adopt a radical apophatic philosophy and insist that *all* and *any* human thought and language is inappropriate, for God (by definition) is beyond and other than thought and language? Doesn't human language impose limitations on God?

There is a sense in which all traditional theists believe God is beyond and other than human thoughts and language. God is beyond both insofar as God (the reality) is not a human thought or term; God pre-existed all human and any other created life. In this sense, God's thoughts are (literally) different from any human thought. In this matter, it is important to keep in mind what philosophers call the difference between *use* and *mention*. If

I *mention* the word 'God' I can report that 'God' consists of three letters, but when I *use* the word 'God' I do not refer to something that consists of three letters. The fact that we are humans and therefore use human language to refer to God does not mean that we cannot use human language to refer to that which is non-human.

Two other replies may be considered.

Defenders of a strict apophatic philosophy of God sometimes assume that conceptual and linguistic limitations are in some sense religiously confining or subjugating. But without concepts or some language, deep religious practices like *loving* or *worshipping God* would be impossible. To love X, you have to have some concept or idea of X. How would you know whether you were or were not worshiping X if you had no idea whatsoever about X? At least in theistic traditions, some language and concept of God seems essential.

Secondly, it should be observed that there is a difference between claiming that *God is more than or greater than our best terms and concepts* and the claim that *God is not less than our best terms and concepts*. So, one may assert that God is omniscient and analyze this in terms of God knowing all that can possibly be known. One may well grant that and yet go on to claim that how God possesses this knowledge and what it would be like to be omniscient surpasses the best possible human imagination.

We will return to the idea that the sacred may be indescribable in chapter 6.

3

Classical and contemporary arguments for God

The most sustained debate in Western philosophy of religion is that between those who assert the reality of God as conceived of generally in the theistic tradition and those who assert that the cosmos itself, or nature, is all that exits. 'Naturalism' is the standard term for the second view. Before considering some positive reasons for embracing theism, it will be useful to get a glimpse of 'the opposition'.

Richard Dawkins offers a useful definition of atheistic naturalism:

> [A] philosophical naturalist is somebody who believes there is nothing beyond the natural, physical world, no *super*natural creative intelligence lurking behind the observable universe, no soul that outlasts the body and no miracles – except in the sense of natural phenomena that we don't yet understand. If there is something that appears to lie beyond the natural world as it is now imperfectly understood, we hope eventually to understand it and embrace it within the natural. As ever when we unweave a rainbow, it will not become less wonderful.

(Dawkins 2006, 14)

Dawkins's naturalism affirms the reality of what he terms the 'natural, physical world' and 'the observable universe', and indeed believes that the world is 'wonderful'. He rules out anything (especially God) 'lurking behind' the cosmos, as well as the soul, an afterlife, and miracles.

Dawkins's characterization of naturalism is a good, representative position, but a technical distinction is worth making. In the literature today, there are two forms of naturalism: *strict naturalism* and *broad naturalism*. The strict naturalist believes that reality consists only of what is described and explained by the ideal natural sciences, especially physics. Many assume that an ideal physics will not include things like subjective experiences or consciousness, ideas, emotions, morality, and the like. This extreme view, claiming that all such mental life does not exist, is sometimes called *eliminativism*. The most well-known eliminativists since the 1960s include Willard van Orman, Quine, Stephen Stitch, Paul and Patricia Churchland, and Daniel Dennett.

In this book, I only take note of strict naturalism as a radical option rather than fully engage it. Strict naturalism faces daunting challenges, beginning with the charge that it is self-refuting because it seems to require its advocates to believe that there are no beliefs and think that there are no thoughts. Their complete rejection of the mental also seems difficult to reconcile with the very existence of science, because science itself is based on systematic observation and experimentation involving experience, thoughts, and reason, among other human phenomena. For a survey and critical evaluation of strict naturalism, see *Naturalism (Interventions)* by Stewart Goetz and myself (2008) or my earlier book *Consciousness and the Mind of God* (2005a).

In the philosophy of religion, a broader naturalism is the key counterpoint to theism and other non-naturalist and religious views of ultimate reality. The broad naturalist grants that there may be thoughts, feelings, emotions, and perhaps even ethical truths. Dawkins, for example, does not deny the reality of thinking: 'Human thoughts and emotions emerge from exceedingly complete interactions of physical entities within the brain'

(Dawkins 2006, 14). But all broad naturalists firmly reject theism. Only the natural exists, and some naturalists, like Matthew Bagger, are quite open about what the natural may include: almost anything but God.

> I intend my use of 'natural' to entail (1) no commitments to a physicalistic ontology; (2) no valorization of the specific methods, vocabularies, presuppositions, or conclusions peculiar to natural science; (3) no view about the reducibility of the mental to the physical; (4) no position on the ontological status of logic or mathematics, and (5) no denial of the possibility of moral knowledge. Beliefs, values, and logical truths, for example, count as natural and folk psychological explanations, therefore, are natural explanations. The concept of the natural, in the sense I use it, has virtually no content except as the definition correlative to the supernatural, taken here as a transcendent order of reality (and causation) distinct from the mundane order presupposed alike by the natural scientist and the rest of us in our quotidian affairs.
>
> (Bagger 1999, 15)

Bagger seems to be one of the broadest of naturalists, allowing for a robust view of the mental and values, so long as theism (or, to use his vocabulary, 'the supernatural') is rejected.

According to either form of naturalism, we have no good reason to believe that reality includes a God. Some naturalists adopt what is called a *presumption of atheism*, according to which if there is no good reason to posit God, one should not do so. Their thinking is very much in line with Ockham's razor, the thesis that one should not posit entities beyond necessity. Dawkins is the most recent in a long line of naturalists who think that if a theist is allowed to posit that God is uncaused, the naturalist should be entitled to adopt the simpler hypothesis that the cosmos is uncaused. On this view, the theist needs to believe in *both* the cosmos *and* God, but if one only has reason to believe the cosmos exists, why posit some additional cosmos-making force?

I consider the case for naturalism in the course of considering four significant, interconnected theistic arguments: the ontological, cosmological, and teleological arguments, and an argument from religious experience. But before we look at these arguments let me make a few general comments about them.

First, I will treat the four arguments in relation to religious theism. The ontological argument contends that reflections on the idea and possibility of God's existence provides a reason for thinking God actually exists. The cosmological argument contends that it is reasonable to think that our contingent cosmos must be accounted for, in part, by the causal creativity of a necessarily existing being. Teleological arguments contend that our ordered, complex cosmos is better explained by theism than by naturalism. And the argument from religious experience argues that the widespread reports by persons across time and culture who experience a transcendent, divine reality provide grounds for thinking there is such a reality. Arguments for theism based on miracles and morality will be addressed in later chapters, and arguments about theism and evil will be the focus of chapter 4.

Second, each of these arguments may support some dimension of the God of the great monotheistic traditions of Judaism, Christianity, Islam, and some forms of Hinduism, but they do so in different ways. The ontological argument, for example, is quite abstract and is usually classified as an a priori argument – an argument that relies largely on reflection rather than observation – whereas the argument from religious experience involves drawing inferences from apparent observations or perceptions.

Third, although the arguments should be considered as independent lines of reasoning, they also should be viewed as interwoven and cumulative. If you only accept the cosmological argument and reject the others, you might believe that there is some kind of necessarily existing reality responsible for the ongoing existence of the cosmos, but no more. However, you might accept two or more of the arguments and find them mutually reinforcing. The cosmological argument may be complemented by a teleological argument, thereby providing reasons for thinking the necessarily existing being is also purposive. Such cumulative reasoning is not unusual. Many of our reasons for important beliefs in science, politics, law, personal relationships, and so on do not rest on a single line of reasoning but on a host of distinguishable, mutually supportive reasons. This multi-dimensional approach to belief has a similar role in philosophy of religion. At certain points, I will indicate how the lines of theistic and naturalist reasoning overlap.

Fourth, a major point to appreciate at the outset is that very few, if any, arguments today in philosophy are considered proofs. There are, rather, good or bad, plausible or implausible, arguments, not decisive proofs or knockout refutations. What I offer are *not* proofs, but they are what I believe are promising arguments notwithstanding the important objections they face.

Fifth, my concern is with comparing two philosophies (theism and naturalism) and the way they provide a comprehensive understanding of reality. The arguments that follow are *categorical* insofar as they appeal to general kinds of things or concepts of reality (the divine nature, the contingency and seemingly purposive character of the cosmos, the apparent experience of the divine) rather than analyze particular problems for otherwise complete theories. As an example of the latter, one might claim that naturalism can explain the complete fossil record except for one missing link, and then appeal to God to explain away the link (e.g. that God created humans as a separate species). This latter line of reasoning has been described as supporting a 'God of the gaps'. Rather than a God of the gaps, the following arguments have a bearing on whether there is a God of the cosmos as a whole.

Finally, there are different versions of the arguments that follow. I have selected those I believe are the most promising, but they are designed for readers to *begin* (rather than wrap up) reflecting on possible arguments and further objections.

Ontological arguments

Although not many philosophers today accept an ontological argument for theism, it does have some formidable defenders and is far more plausible than the standard introductions to the philosophy of religion admit. We will spend time on it in order to address a key thesis advanced by some naturalists: that the cosmos itself may be as equally self-explaining, or as basic, as God.

One promising version of the ontological argument begins with an elucidation of the concept of God as a maximally excellent reality. Contemporary advocates of perfect being theology, who trace its roots back to Anselm of Canterbury (1033–1109), contend that a being of maximal excellence will have the attributes of necessary existence, consciousness, benevolence, and limitless intentional power and knowledge.

This Anselmian idea of God has some intuitive plausibility. Imagine any great excellence, from the birth of a galaxy to romantic love. What would be better than such things? A *being* who could intentionally create them. Remove any of the above attributes and the being would be less than maximally excellent. A non-conscious divine reality would not have any powers to create or act intentionally, let alone have purposes or a good will, for example, and a being that existed contingently would lack an excellence of a being whose essence involves existence.

Let us now consider how this Anselmian concept of God has been used to foster an ontological argument for God's existence. Given the above understanding of divine attributes, the first premise of an ontological argument may be formulated as:

1. God either exists necessarily or God's existence is impossible. This premise is based on the supposition that if God exists, God does not exist contingently but necessarily. An analogy may be useful: Take the propositions $2 + 2 = 4$ and $2 + 2 = 6$. The first is *necessarily* true, not probably right or accidentally right. 2 is $1 + 1$ and 4 is $1 + 1 + 1 + 1$, so the proposition simply states the necessary truth that $1 + 1 + 1 + 1 = 1 + 1 + 1 + 1$. $2 + 2 = 6$, however, is *necessarily* false. Its falsehood is not a matter of contingency.

Before proceeding, let us consider a foundational objection sometimes advanced to prevent the argument from being launched. The philosopher Immanuel Kant (1724–1804) famously argued that 'existence' or 'being' does not name a real property or (in his terminology) 'predicate.' He writes, '*Being* [or existence] is obviously not a real predicate; that is, it is not a concept of something which could be added to the concept of a thing' (Kant 1950 [1781], 504–5). Brian and Beverly Clack elaborate,

> This is a crucial point: existence is not a predicate, and as such it cannot be a perfection. Existence tells us something about an object, rather than something about *the nature of* that object. To say that something exists adds nothing to the description of an object, but rather says that there is an instance of such an object in the world. Descartes [who, like Anselm, thought of God as necessarily existing] had felt that 'exists' functioned logically like 'is omnipotent' or 'is brown'; that it told us something about the nature of a thing. To see the confused character of that thought, though, imagine the following

situation. In a state of thirst, I enter a bar. This exchange now takes place:

Clack: Can I have a drink please?

Barman: What kind of drink would you like?

Clack: Oh, an existing one, please.

(Clack and Clack 2008, 17)

But these observations do not address the crucial starting point of the ontological argument: There is a distinction between different modes of existing. Some things exist contingently, like the drink Clack orders. But other things exist necessarily, like mathematical properties and the laws of logic. To object to the ontological argument on the grounds that it treats *existence* as a property is therefore wholly unconvincing. If we had compelling reasons to believe that there could be no such thing as *existing necessarily* (which could be the equivalent to believing that necessary existence is impossible), then the ontological argument would fail. But so far no one has presented compelling reasons.

Back to the argument. The next premise is as follows:

2. God's existence is possible.

This premise has been, and is being, debated at length by philosophers. A range of atheists contend that God's existence is impossible. The most recent effort is the collection of essays *The Impossibility of God*, edited by Michael Martin, in which many different philosophers seek to show that any reasonable concept of God involves a contradiction. These arguments are akin to those considered in chapter 2 denying that a being can be omniscient and incorporeal or omnipotent and essentially good. A defense of the ontological argument would need to show that these objections can be met. As it happens, I think they can be, and have been, met and that no current argument has established God's impossibility. But because of the controversial nature of premise 2, let us not move ahead hastily.

A defense of the second premise may need a principle of evidence such as the following:

> It is reasonable to believe that a state of affairs (SOA) is possible if there are no compelling reasons for thinking the SOA is impossible and it appears that the SOA can be imagined or conceived or consistently described.

Many SOAs will turn out not to pass this standard. The following SOAs cannot be consistently described and involve a contradiction or an apparent impossibility: a square circle (an object that both has and does not have four right triangles), $1 + 1 = 3$, a color that does not take up space (colors like redness seem to require some spatial extension whether it be an afterimage, hallucination, or the surface of an apple). But some SOAs may be seen to be possible even if they never actually exist: a restaurant ten miles long, a unicorn, extraterrestrials, and so on. Imagining such SOAs is customarily referred to as conducting a *thought experiment*. It has been argued that thought experiments have an indispensable role in both philosophical and non-philosophical inquiry (Sorenson 1992).

Let us now consider premise 3.

3. It is not impossible that God exists.
This seems to follow, given the first two premises. If a SOA is impossible then it is simply *not* possible. But if a SOA is possible, it is not impossible. We then reach the fourth premise:

4. God's existence is necessary.
This follows directly from the first and third premises. If the only alternatives are *God existing necessarily* or *God's existence is impossible* and impossibility is ruled out, then God must exist necessarily. We are left with the conclusion:

5. Therefore God exists.

There are many objections and replies to consider, but let's focus on two: the perfect island objection, and the possible non-existence of God objection.

The perfect island objection

Some philosophers object that the ontological argument could be used to justify any number of SOAs, including imaginary ones. A perfect island would have beautiful sand, water, trees, abundant yet ecologically stable life, beautiful people, and so on. And it would *necessarily* exist. If so, the argument can be made:

1. Either a perfect island exists necessarily or it is impossible.
2. It is possible that a perfect island exists. After all, we know of no reason why it cannot, and we seem to be able to imagine, conceive, or consistently describe one.
3. A perfect island is not impossible.
4. A perfect island exists necessarily.
5. A perfect island exists.

According to this objection, the ontological argument might also justify the perfect magician, the perfect unicorn, and anything else. The ontological argument should be rejected if it leads to such absurdities.

The classic reply to this objection is that a perfect island is a contingent thing. An island is something we might hope to discover but not something whose existence is impossible. In brief, the objection does not take seriously the at least *apparent* uniqueness of the concept of God. What would be better than a perfect island? Perhaps an island-maker who can create and sustain indefinitely such landmasses in endless water with ever changing but sustainable ecology.

There is one other, more offbeat reply to this objection. Let's say the objector insists that an island does indeed have all great-making properties. Well, compare two islands: an island with a conscious mind, like the one that appears in the popular television series *Lost*, and one without. Wouldn't the one with consciousness have an excellence the other lacks? Now imagine the minded island possessed omniscience, essential goodness, omnipresence, and perfect power. Wouldn't these, too, be excellences? My point is that if one tries to use the concept of an island as the concept of unsurpassable excellence, the 'island' will cease being a literal, recognizable island and instead become a metaphor or image for a divine being akin to the God of perfect being theology. (A perfect being theologian might poetically use the concept of God being like an island – a place of refuge, for example – just as God has been described metaphorically as a mighty rock, a foundation, a fountain, a good shepherd, and the like.)

The possible non-existence of God objection

This objection challenges premise 2 with the counter-claim, 'It is possible that God does not exist.' It holds that we can imagine, conceive, and consistently describe a cosmos in which God does not exist. If we can conceive of a Godless world, isn't it reasonable to believe that God might not exist? If that is true, then God's existence is *not* necessary, hence it is impossible that God exists.

Two points are worth considering in reply. First, if it is indeed possible God does not exist, in virtue of *what* is God's existence impossible? An impossible states of affairs (e.g. the square circle) is impossible by virtue of a contradiction in terms or evident incoherence. In the case of God, is there any such contradiction? Only contradiction or incoherence can find a meaningful chink in the armor of this logical framework and a decisive argument that there is such contradiction or incoherence has not been presented.

Second, what is involved in conceiving of God's possible non-existence? I can conceive of the absence of all sorts of things by imagining a world that excludes them. I can imagine an island or continent or world without elephants. But could I imagine a cosmos in which there is no *incorporeal* God? I suggest that to secure the premise that it is possible that God does not exist, one would have also to *entertain* the concept of God and conceive of God not existing in reality. But imagining that God possibly does not exist is difficult, especially if we lack an argument that God's existence is impossible. My picturing a world without God would be like my picturing a world while not picturing God. But this gives one no reason to conclude it is possible God does not exist – I can conceive of a world without conceiving of $1 + 1 = 2$, but this gives me no reason for thinking it is possible that $1 + 1$ does not equal 2.

A different example may be useful. Imagine someone, Smith, who thinks he can imagine water without imagining H_2O. He has developed a thought experiment in which he observes water in a glass in front of him that retains all its observable qualities as water (the liquid is still colorless and odorless, it boils at 100 degrees Celsius, and so on), even after a chemist has removed all the hydrogen and oxygen atoms. Should this thought experiment lead us to believe you can have water without H_2O? Presumably not. The *essence* of water *is* H_2O. Defenders of the ontological argument similarly reason that existence is the *essence* of God, and apparent thought experiments of God not existing are in the same boat as Smith's thought experiment.

A general point about *possibility* should be noted. The ontological argument concerns what it is reasonable to believe, in terms of what is possible, necessary, and impossible. But we also use the word 'possible' to refer to our degree of certainty. So, someone entertaining a complex mathematical conjecture might say, 'It is possible that it is true,' but mean, 'For all I know, it is true; after all, it has worked so far.' But the conjecture is either necessary or impossible (i.e. either true or false), but not anywhere in between, so it is not a merely contingent matter. Some people treat the ontological argument like Goldbach's conjecture (every even number is the sum of two prime numbers) which has not yet been proven true and allow that the first premise stands: God's existence is either necessary or impossible. Philosophers might then diverge, some contending that it seems likely (reasonable) that God's existence is impossible, others arguing that it is likely (reasonable) that God's existence is necessary, and still other philosophers uncommitted.

Although the ontological argument has never enjoyed wide popularity, almost every generation of philosophers since its development in the eleventh century until today has included a serious and respected defender of the argument. The next three theistic arguments have enjoyed greater support.

Cosmological arguments

There are many forms of the cosmological argument. Cosmological arguments raise the question about the very nature of the cosmos itself. It appears, from science and our ordinary reasoning about ourselves and the world, that events occur for a reason and, moreover, that you and I, the planet, and the galaxy exist for a reason. Events and objects seem to depend for their existence on other events and objects. Most (but not all) cosmological arguments begin with the question of why our cosmos exists rather than not exist. This may take the form of asking why there is a cosmos at all rather than empty space, or asking why our cosmos exists rather than some other cosmos.

I present in what follows a prominent version of the argument derived, in part, from the English philosopher Samuel Clarke (1675–1729) and developed in the twentieth century by the American philosopher Richard Taylor. Taylor introduces his version of the cosmological argument by asking us to imagine that we are walking in the woods and find something unusual, a smooth and clear ball about our own height.

> You would deem this puzzling and mysterious, certainly, but if one considers the matter, it is no more inherently mysterious that such a thing should exist than that anything else should exist. If you were quite accustomed to finding such objects of various sizes around you most of the time, but had never seen an ordinary rock, then upon finding a large rock in the woods one day you would be just as puzzled and mystified. This illustrates the fact that something that is mysterious ceases to seem so simply by its accustomed presence. It is strange indeed, for example, that a world such as ours should exist; yet few people are very often struck by this strangeness but simply take it for granted.

Though we might be mystified by the ball, he continues,

> there is one thing you would hardly question; namely, that it did not appear there all by itself, that it owes its existence to something. You might not have the remotest idea whence and how it came to be there, but you would hardly doubt that there was an explanation. The idea that it might have come from nothing at all, that it might exist without there being any explanation of its existence, is one that few people would consider worthy of entertaining.

(Taylor 1974, 103–4)

Taylor contends that this thought experiment brings to light a principle of sufficient reason. With respect to *anything* in the cosmos we reasonably suppose that there is some reason why it exists rather than not. This question is not answered, according to Taylor, by claiming that the cosmos has always existed.

It should now be noted that it is no answer to the question, why a thing exists, to state *how long* it has existed. A geologist does not suppose that she has explained why there should be rivers and mountains merely by pointing out that they are old. Similarly, if one were to ask, concerning the ball of which we have spoken, for some sufficient reason for its being, he would not receive any answer upon being told that it had been there since yesterday. Nor would it be any better answer to say that it had existed since before anyone could remember, or even that it had always existed; for the question was not one concerning its age, but its existence. If, to be sure, one were to ask where a given thing came from, or how it came into being, then upon learning that it had always existed he would learn that it never really *came* into being at all; but he could still reasonably wonder why it should exist at all.

(Taylor 1974, 106–7)

We now come to the crux of the cosmological argument: in a cosmos such as ours that appears to be contingent (not necessary), what might provide a sufficient reason that it exists rather than not? If the cosmos is contingent, there will never be a sufficient reason, for to account for a contingent being by means of another contingent being (and so on to infinity) can never give us a reason why any contingent being exists.

An analogy may be useful. Imagine I give you the word 'omishimiliga' (a term I just made up) and you ask me what it means, and I then give you another word you have never heard of: 'ariljsehr'. I could go on and on making up words, but unless you can break out of the series of unknown terms to a word you know you will never know the meaning of 'omishimiliga'.

Some philosophers, however, claim that an infinite series explains why any contingent being exists. Paul Edwards develops this point with an illustration explaining how a series of books can be supported.

A *finite* series of books would ... come crashing down, since the first or lowest member would not have a predecessor on which it could be supported. If the series, however, were infinite this would not be the case. In that event every member *would* have a predecessor to support itself on and there would be no crash. That is to say: a crash can be avoided ... by an infinite series.

(Edwards 1974, 76–7)

The analogy seems strained. If each book provides a reason the book above it is suspended in space (or, by analogy, why it exists), we are still unable, by appealing just to similarly dependent, contingent things, to explain why *any* book is suspended (or exists) or why there should be any books at all rather than no books.

The cosmological argument, then, holds that a necessarily existing being whose activity explains the very existence and continuance of the cosmos avoids the problem of positing an infinity of contingent explanations and maintains our widespread, evident, and practical belief that events occur and things exist for a reason. F.R. Copleston summarizes the main strategy of the cosmological argument as showing 'that what we call the world is intrinsically unintelligible, apart from the existence of God'.

You see, I don't believe that the infinity of the series of events – I mean a horizontal series, so to speak – if such an infinity could be proved, would be in the slightest degree relevant to the situation. If you add up chocolates you get chocolates after all and not a sheep. If you add up chocolates to infinity, you presumably get an infinite number of chocolates. So if you add up contingent beings to infinity, you still get contingent beings, not a necessary being. An infinite series of contingent beings will be, to my way of thinking, as unable to cause itself as one contingent being.

(Copleston in Russell 1957, 139)

On this view, no matter how complex our empirical science, so long as the cosmos is seen to be contingent there will be a failure to reach a complete explanation of the cosmos. In his recent defense of the cosmological argument, Timothy O'Connor points out that explaining the existence of a contingent cosmos by appealing to a necessarily existing being is something that can ground, or form a basis for, our explanations of things within the cosmos.

> If our universe truly is contingent, the obtaining of certain fundamental facts or other will be unexplained within empirical theory, whatever the topological structure of contingent reality. An infinite regress of beings in or outside the spatiotemporal universe cannot forestall such a result. If there is to be an ultimate, or complete, explanation, it will have to ground in some way the most fundamental, contingent facts of the universe in a necessary being, something which has the reason for its existence within its own nature. It bears emphasis that such an unconditional explanation need not in any way compete with conditional, empirical explanations. Indeed, it is natural to suppose that empirical explanations will be subsumed within the larger structure of the complete explanation.
>
> (O'Connor 2008, 76)

A good way to test this argument is to assess it in light of objections. Consider the following series of questions and objections.

Why think the necessary cause is God? Why couldn't the necessary cause be the cosmos itself? These questions are at work in Dawkins's critique of theism. Dawkins argues that cosmological arguments

> rely upon the idea of a regress and invoke God to terminate it. They make the entirely unwarranted assumption that God himself is immune to the regress. Even if we allow the dubious

luxury of arbitrarily conjuring up a terminator to an infinite regress and giving it a name, simply because we need one, there is absolutely no reason to endow that terminator with any of the properties normally ascribed to God: omnipotence, omniscience, goodness, creativity of design, to say nothing of such human attributes as listening to prayers, forgiving sins and reading innermost thoughts.

(Dawkins 2006, 77)

Several replies are in order.

First, the cosmological argument as we have considered it here does not endeavor to establish *all* the divine attributes. The argument is only that without a necessarily existing (not contingent) being the existence of a contingent cosmos is unexplained. The reason for recognizing the causal contribution of a necessarily existing being is not to conjure up a convenient terminator of regress. The reason is that without one we cannot account for the contingent cosmos. This is not an example of 'conjuring' and arbitrary positing of a convenient entity.

Second, though Dawkins rejects the significance of this argument for a full philosophy of God, an argument that the natural world requires a transcendent cause is itself quite dramatic (to put it mildly) and would or should worry the atheist. Although philosophers usually use teleological arguments to provide reasons for thinking there is an *intentional* account of the cosmos, a successful cosmological argument itself may give us grounds for positing that the necessary being has agency. To account for why *this* cosmos exists and is sustained rather than a different one or none at all, the necessary cause must differentiate between possible states of affairs.

Let us consider this point very briefly and then return to objections and questions. Imagine that the only spatiotemporal object that exists is like the tiny planet of the little prince in Antoine de Saint-Exupéry's novella *Le Petit Prince*. On the planet there are three volcanoes, baobab trees, a rose, and the prince. Imagine (for the sake of argument) that the cosmological argument successfully establishes that the existence and sustained continuance must be accounted for by a necessarily existing being. One reason for thinking this cause must be intentional is that in order to account for why *that* planet exists (with all its precise contents) rather than another, its fundamental constituents would need to be causally sustained. Why wouldn't one cosmos cease and another take its place with four volcanoes and two roses? A natural account would attribute this to the intentions of a creative cause, just as the natural account would explain why Saint-Exupéry's book contains a planet with three volcanoes, baobab trees, and a rose, by the intentions of the author.

Does this introduction of personal agency wreak havoc with the concept of natural laws of nature? Not at all, as we shall see when we look at teleological arguments. Cosmological and teleological arguments provide reasons for why there is a cosmos at all. They offer not a *scientific* explanation of the cosmos, but a *philosophical* explanation. The arguments should (if successful) account for the fact that we live in a cosmos where science is successful. Science involves empirical inquiry, repeatable experiments, and so on, whereas a philosophical explanation, in this case, involves reflection upon why there is and continues to be a contingent cosmos at all.

But if the cosmological argument goes beyond science, isn't it going beyond what we have any right or ability to explore? Consider this exchange between Bertrand Russell and F.R. Copleston:

RUSSELL: But when is an explanation adequate? Suppose I am about to make a flame with a match. You may say that the adequate explanation of that is that I rub it on the box.

COPLESTON: Well, for practical purposes – but theoretically, that is only a partial explanation. An adequate explanation must ultimately be a total explanation, to which nothing further can be added.

RUSSELL: Then I can only say that you're looking for something which can't be got, and which one ought not to expect to get.

COPLESTON: To say that one has not found it is one thing; to say that one should not look for it seems to me rather dogmatic.

(Russell 1957, 138)

We may *like* the cosmos to have a comprehensive explanation, but we face the challenge J.L. Mackie put succinctly: 'We have no right to assume that the universe will comply with our intellectual preferences' (Mackie 1983, 86–7).

In reply, I suggest that if it is quite in line with our drive to ask for explanations *within the cosmos*, then it also seems natural and plausible to ask about *an explanation of the cosmos as a whole*. If one can make sense of the concept of a necessarily existing being, it is hard to resist the intuitive, core driving force of cosmological reasoning. It is at this point that a defender of the cosmological argument might draw on the ontological argument. The ontological argument may well not succeed in persuading anyone to adopt theism, but it at least elucidates and clarifies the idea of a necessarily existing, unsurpassably excellent being.

Even if the cosmological argument succeeds, why does the cosmos have only one necessary cause? Why not three or a hundred?

Two replies may be considered. First, one might re-formulate the argument to the effect that there is at least one necessary cause. One may then appeal to the favorite device of most naturalists: Ockham's razor. If you do not need to posit additional entities, do not do so. A second reply draws on the ontological argument to contend that we possess a unique concept of a necessarily existing being with causal power.

Consider one other, more popular objection: if one is going to explain properly the contingency of the cosmos, doesn't one need to appeal to a necessary cause? But this raises the following difficulty. If God's creating and sustaining the cosmos is necessary, then it appears not to be a free action. This creates a problem, for most theists believe that God's creation was free. And a related problem exists if one concedes that God's creation was not free, but necessary. If God's creating is necessary, then the cosmos is necessary and not contingent after all.

To reply to this objection takes us to the teleological argument. Theists usually reply that the explanation for the cosmos lies in the intentional, purposive good will of the creator. The problem of explaining why the cosmos exists is resolved (so it is argued) by appeal to a necessarily existing being who freely wills that there be a cosmos. The *reality* of God does not need additional explaining, and God's intentional activity is itself to be understood in terms of reasons and purposes. The reasons and purposes are believed by theists to account for (but not necessitate) the free will of the creator. To get a fuller idea of this order of explanation, let us turn to the teleological argument.

Teleological arguments

We now reach a popular argument historically and culturally that lies behind theism: the apparent value and purposive nature of the cosmos provides some reason to believe there is an intentional, powerful, good, and creative reality that creates and sustains it. This argument has also been the subject of rigorous criticism. Before presenting the argument in a positive format, consider two objections that may prevent the argument from getting off the ground.

Objection 1: Theistic explanations by their very nature are empty or void of significance. Matthew Bagger has proposed that we simply cannot *ever* resort to theistic accounts: '[W]e can never assert that, in principle, an event resists naturalistic explanation. In the modern age in actual inquiry, we never reach the point where we throw up our hands and appeal to divine intervention to explain a localized event like an extraordinary experience' (Bagger 1999, 13).

Bagger appeals to what we moderns assume in all other contexts of explanation, and none of these seems to allow for an appeal to God (or what Bagger calls 'the supernatural'). Jan Narveson offers a more pointed, direct assault on theistic explanations, which he sees as empty of content. They are empty of content because they fail to account for *how* God's will is efficacious. It is no explanation at all to suppose that 'some infinitely powerful mind simply willed it thus and … ho!, it was so!'

> If we are serious about 'natural theology,' then we ought to be ready to supply content in our explication of theological hypotheses just as we do when we explicate scientific hypotheses. Such explications carry the brunt of explanations. Why does water boil when heated? The scientific story supplies an analysis of matter in its liquid state, the effects of atmospheric pressure and heat, and so on until we see, in impressive detail, just how the thing works. An explanation's right to be called 'scientific' is, indeed, in considerable part earned precisely by its ability to provide such detail.
>
> (Narveson 2003, 93–4)

If Narveson and Bagger are correct, a theistic explanation of the cosmos is not a live option.

Objection 2: Hasn't the Darwinian theory of evolution shown that a cosmos that appears to be purposive or designed was produced by non-purposive, non-intelligent forces? Darwinian evolution posits that random changes give rise to mutations in a species and that through natural processes species members that do not adapt are selected against. Over extensive periods of change, organisms with powers of vision, thought, emotion, and so on evolve. Darwin himself was initially impressed by a teleological argument developed by William Paley who argued that the cosmos resembles objects we know to be designed like clocks. If the cosmos resembles a clock or other known artifacts, shouldn't we conclude that the cosmos itself is an artifact and thus has a designer? But Darwin later came to conclude that the seemingly intentional character of the cosmos can be the outcome of mindless forces, given enough time. Darwin writes,

> The old argument of design in nature, as given by Paley, which formerly seemed to me so conclusive, fails, now that the law of natural selection has been discovered. We can no longer argue that, for instance, the beautiful hinge of a bivalve shell must have been made by an intelligent being, like the hinge of a door by man. There seems to be no more design in the variability of organic beings and in the action of natural selection, than in the course which the wind blows.

> (Darwin 2002 [1876], 50)

In reply, it is not my intent to fully endorse a teleological argument here, but I do hope to offer a sufficient defense that the argument may be taken seriously.

Against Narveson and Bagger, one may reply that there are two general kinds of explanations for events: intentional accounts (which *invoke* values, designs, purposes) and non-intentional accounts (which *lack* values, designs, and purposes). For example, accounts of heat, light, gravity, and chemical bonds scientifically consist of non-intentional causal explanations. An account of the speed of light contains no recourse to desire, purpose, or value. Intentional explanations are essential, however, if one wants to explain my writing and your reading of this book. Some eliminativists (the strict naturalists discussed earlier) have proposed that *all* explanations must (in the end) avoid intentionality, but I shall assume (as most philosophers today hold) that an account of your reading must include some beliefs, desires, and intentions (a curiosity about religion, a desire to think critically about it, and so on).

If there are such intentional explanations, there must be what some philosophers call *basic actions*. These are acts one does for reasons but directly and without the mediation of other acts. I might do one thing (get your attention) by doing another (calling out to you), but some acts are not mediated. My calling out to you because I want to meet you may require a host of factors to come into play in a full explanation (factors including social expectations, language use, personality type, etc.). But some acts will be not further accountable by other acts. When I called, I did not do so by my willing that certain neurons fire, my nervous system react in some way, and so on – I simply did the act. When Narveson complains that theistic explanation lacks certain mechanisms and causal elements, his complaint would cut against intentional explanations in ordinary human (and other animal) activities. In everyday, bona fide explanations of human agency, there are basic acts that are not further reducible into 'impressive detail'. (It should also be noted that if there must always be an answer to 'how things work' in physical causation, there can be no basic physical causes. This seems counter to many views of causation in the physical world and threatens an infinite regress.) If divine intentions are basic, so are some human intentions even though the latter are exercised by beings with animal bodies. Hence, I think Narveson is not successful in ruling out the possibility of theistic accounts.

If Narveson is not successful, it is hard to see that Bagger is either. In his characterization of naturalism cited at the start of this chapter, he explicitly does *not* commit himself to materialism or to the emptiness of intentional explanations. If he allows intentional explanations in principle, it is difficult to see why an appeal to our 'modern' sensibilities and values can exclude theism in principle. Recall Bagger's treatment of what is natural. His use of 'natural' is one of the widest I know, for it appears that his definition allows for a natural world that is radically non-materialistic (perhaps even idealism, according to which reality consists of mental states) or pan-psychic (the view that all of reality has mental properties), so long as God is not included. But if the natural can include such capacious reference to the mental and the intentional, how can it rule out, as a general principle, an appeal to divine intentionality?

On evolution

There are versions of the teleological argument that challenge evolutionary theory. In the intelligent design movement, for example, it is argued that there are signs of irreducible complexity in biology that require explanation in terms of design. There is not space to fully explore this option here, so I note more generally that a teleological argument can grant a comprehensive Darwinian account of evolution and then ask why there is a cosmos in which evolution takes place. Richard Swinburne invites such a broader view, in which the task is to explain evolution itself along with the cosmos as a whole.

> For an ultimate explanation we need an explanation at the highest level of why those laws rather than any other ones operated. The laws of evolution are no doubt consequences of laws of chemistry governing the organic matter of which animals are made. And the laws of chemistry hold because fundamental laws of physics hold. But why just those fundamental laws of physics rather than any others? If the laws of physics did not have the consequence that some chemical arrangement would give rise to life, or that there would be random variations of offspring from characteristics of parents, and so on, there would be no

evolution by natural selection. So, even given that there are laws of nature (i.e. that material objects have the same powers and liabilities as each other), why just those laws?

(Swinburne 1996, 60)

There is some reason, then, to think that Darwinian evolution has not refuted the teleological argument.

Let us now consider a constructive version of the teleological argument.

Is the cosmos fundamentally good? Treatments of good and evil will concern us further in chapter 5 on the problem of evil and in chapter 7. For now, let's assume a common sense or ordinary notion of good wherein something is good (roughly) if it is worthy of pursuing or enjoying or admiring or praising. Theists have pointed to the goodness of there being a contingent cosmos at all, one with stable laws of nature; they consider the emergence of life good, as well as the emergence of human and non-human beings with powers of motion, sensation, perception, desire, emotion, reason, and memory. They further recognize as good the emergence not just of consciousness, but of free agency and moral, religious, and aesthetic awareness. The argument then poses this question: does theism or its most powerful competitor, naturalism, provide the better explanation for this good, contingent cosmos? If naturalism is true, and the most fundamental forms of explanation are non-intentional, then the goodness of the cosmos is not part of an account of why this cosmos exists. There is no antecedent or independent reason that is generated in naturalism that there should be a good cosmos – the goodness of the cosmos is a mere accident or non-intended consequence of impersonal forces. If theism is correct, however, and there is a good, powerful, all-knowing, intentional being, then that being will have a reason for creating a good cosmos. According to theism, part of the reason why the cosmos exists is its goodness.

Before getting to objections and replies, consider an analogy to help fill out the argument. Imagine you come across what seems to be writing on a beach which reads, 'Beware of sharks.' The marks in the sand are not very clear, however, and some of what appear to be letters may have been caused by random waves. Consider two hypotheses: on one account you are seeing letters deliberately fashioned to warn you about danger; on a second account you are seeing something utterly random that happens to resemble a warning in English. Perhaps you decide to withhold judgment but then think that you see a shark just offshore. At that point it would be reasonable to conclude that the marks were made by an intentional, good agent. If agency is involved then the fact that the marks formed into a warning is part of the explanation of why the warning is there, whereas if agency is not involved the resemblance to writing is accidental in the same way that a cloud formation might look like a duck.

Now consider four objections and replies.

The objection from simplicity

Dawkins has raised the objection that teleological and design arguments fail because they have to posit a highly complex cause of the cosmos. Naturalistic evolutionary explanations are preferable because they begin with simple components and explain the emergence of life et al. incrementally. Theists are completely out of step with proper scientific explanations that explain the complex in terms of the simple. To posit a God as your chief explanatory cause is

> tantamount to dealing yourself a perfect hand of bridge ... To suggest that the first cause, the great unknown which is responsible for something existing rather than nothing, is a being capable of designing the universe and of talking to a million people simultaneously, is a total abdication of the responsibility

to find an explanation. It is a dreadful exhibition of self-indulgent, thought-denying skyhookery.

(Dawkins 2006, 155)

What is missing in Dawkins's objection is an understanding of the uniqueness of the concept of God as a necessarily existing, maximally excellent being. The concept of God is not the concept of a complex subject with arbitrarily designated properties, but of a simple being whose essential goodness leads God to create the cosmos because such a creation is good. As far as simplicity goes, theism offers a uniquely singular framework. Recall that theism is *not a scientific hypothesis*. So, theists do not (or do not *generally*) appeal to complex individual divine acts in accounting for specific events, e.g. whether the earth came into being 4.5 billion years ago. Theism may be seen as an ideal form of *intentional explanation* (rather than many intentional agents of different powers, there is a single powerful agent) whereas Dawkins's naturalism is an ideal case of a non-intentional framework. The teleological argument then asks which is able to account better for the goodness of the cosmos, contending that theism does a better job than naturalism. There is nothing in principle self-indulgent or thought-denying in comparing theism and naturalism as general philosophies of nature and arguing that theism offers a wider, more successful account.

The objection from uniqueness

The teleological argument asks us to consider the best account of the cosmos as a whole. This is an utterly unique object of inquiry and we lack the means of adjudicating such a quest for explanations. If, as Charles Peirce once suggested, universes were as plentiful as blackberries, we might compare our own universe with universes we know were created and those we know were not, and thus determine the probability that our universe is created, but this level of comparison is not possible (O'Hear 1984, 116–17).

One theistic reply is that if we rule out inferences in such unique, abstract cases, then we have to rule out otherwise perfectly respectable scientific accounts of the origin of the cosmos. An objection against theism here would seem to work equally well against contemporary cosmology in physics. Besides, though it is not possible to compare the layout of different cosmic histories as if we were examining a series of blackberries, it is, in principle, possible to envisage alternative possible worlds. Some of these may be chaotic or random or work on the basis of laws that cripple the emergence of life. These worlds may still be worlds we can envisage an intelligent being creating, but in considering their features we may be able to articulate more fully what counts as evidence of purposive design that should lead us to conclude that it was designed as opposed to created at random or not created at all. (Peirce thought the cosmos to be an intentional creation of a loving force.)

The infinity objection

Perhaps the teleological argument has force if we think of the cosmos as having a short finite past. But if we allow infinite time it seems that the cosmos will eventually produce something that looks designed. It's been suggested that if you provide an infinite number of monkeys with infinite computers or typewriters and infinite time, they would eventually produce the complete works of Shakespeare. (Actually, you would only need one monkey and a computer, for, given infinite time, the monkey would produce no less than two or infinitely many monkeys.) The teleological argument loses ground once one posits a beginningless cosmos because it is now probable (or certain?) that at some point the cosmos will appear to be designed.

William L. Craig and other philosophers have pointed out the many paradoxes that arise in positing actual infinities. Infinity works well in mathematics and in positing potential infinites; a potential infinite is a series that continues without end but is never complete. We can imagine a deathless person counting numbers, beginning with one and counting for ever, but we cannot properly imagine them completing the task and reaching the greatest possible number or having counted sequentially all numbers. Consider just one paradox about actual infinites. Imagine you have an infinite library with infinitely many books that are numbered from one on, ad infinitum. Imagine someone checks out every hundredth book. How many books were checked out? If there is an infinity of books in the library, will there be any fewer books in the library after infinitely many have been checked out? If the original library had an actual infinity of books, it would have no fewer books. Now check out another infinite number of books – those divisible by three. Again, there would be no fewer books in the library. Because of paradoxes like this, some philosophers conclude that there can be no actual infinites. By their lights, the concept of infinity is like the concept of negative numbers – both have a role in mathematics but neither refers to objects in the 'real world' (Craig, in Craig and Smith 1993, 12).

Even if we allow for a cosmos with no beginning and thus an infinite past, a different reply is in the offing. If, given infinity, virtually any cosmos would emerge (many of which, or maybe infinitely many of which, would appear designed), wouldn't this argument undermine most of our ordinary reasoning about ourselves and the world? Perhaps, given infinity, one cosmos might be produced in which you are the only conscious being but you are surrounded by, and live with, humanoids – beings who are exactly like yourself in constitution and behavior but lack consciousness. Some philosophers have argued that this is a possible state of affairs, and, if it is possible, and given infinity all bona fide possibilities will occur, perhaps you should suspend judgment about whether the apparent people around you are genuinely conscious rather than zombies. The appeal to infinity (if there can be actual infinities) does assist an objection to the teleological argument, just as Darwin's theory of evolution was assisted in the nineteenth century by positing an older earth. The only problem is that if appeal to infinity will get you a reason to believe the cosmos will take any number of possible forms, then it appears that much of our reasoning about the cosmos will be undermined along with the teleological argument. The latter argument takes the appearance of purposive value and the greater explanatory power of theism as a reason in support of theism as opposed to naturalism. If positing infinity undermines that, why wouldn't it also undermine our conclusions about science and history in which we must reject appearances because, given infinite galaxies and time, it is possible that such appearances may occur and yet all be false?

Objection: Is the cosmos good? It contains so much evil that it is more likely the result of blind, non-intentional forces than an essentially good being.

Reply: This objection is so significant that the whole of chapter 5 will be dedicated to reflections about the goodness and evil of the cosmos.

An argument from religious experience

Let us consider a widespread reason that is appealed to for theistic and other religious beliefs: the apparent experiential encounter with a transcendent, sacred reality. An example of a religious experience might be a good place to start. Here is a description from William James's *The Varieties of Religious Experience*:

All at once I experienced a feeling of being raised above myself, I felt the presence of God – I tell of the thing just as I was conscious of it – as if his goodness and his power were penetrating me altogether … I sat down on a stone, unable to stand any longer, and my eyes overflowed with tears … Then, slowly, the ecstasy left my heart; that is, I felt that God had withdrawn the communion which he had granted, and I was able to walk on … The impression had been so profound that in climbing slowly the slope I asked myself if it were possible that Moses on Sinai could have had a more intimate communication with God. I think it well to add that in the ecstasy of mine God had neither form, color, odor, nor taste; moreover, that the feeling of his presence was accompanied with no determinate localization … At bottom the expression most apt to render what I felt is this: God was present, though invisible; he fell under no one of my senses, yet my consciousness perceived him.

(James 1960 [1902], 82–83)

There are a host of such reports found in many if not most cultures. Shouldn't such reports be trusted unless there is very good reason to override them? Some outstanding philosophers believe that trust is in order (Jerome Gellman, Richard Swinburne, Gary Gutting, William Wainwright, William Alston, Caroline Davis, and Keith Yandell). Yandell, like many other philosophers, contends that religious experience (which he refers to as 'numinous experience') resembles perceptual experience of objects. We trust the latter, so why not trust the former? Yandell writes,

If there is experiential evidence for any existential proposition, perceptual experiences provide evidence that there are physical objects; it is arbitrary not to add that perceptual experience provides evidence that God exists, unless there is some epistemically relevant difference between sensory and numinous experience. The crucial similarities are that both sorts of experience are 'intentional' and have phenomenologies, or can be expressed via 'intentional' phenomenological descriptions. That perceptual experiences have sensory fillings or phenomenologies, and numinous experiences do not, by itself seems no more reason to think that numinous experience in no way supports the proposition *There is a God* than does the fact that numinous experiences have theistic fillings or phenomenologies, and perceptual experiences do not, by itself provides reason for thinking that perceptual experience in no way supports the proposition *There are physical objects*.

(Yandell 1984, 11)

Consider three strong objections.

Objection 1: Religious (or numinous) experiences are different from perceptual experiences. We can confirm perceptual experiences that are open to public verification, but there is no checking on religious experience. Michael Martin writes,

For example, in order to be able to justify my spontaneous perceptual belief that there is a brown table in front of me, it would seem necessary in principle to be able to argue thus: Spontaneous beliefs of a certain sort occurring under certain conditions are usually true, and my belief that there is a brown table in front of me is of this sort and occurs under these conditions. Consequently, my belief is probably true.

(Martin 1990, 156)

Reply 1: One radical response would be to press a skeptical objection against perceptual experience. Sure, we do rely on perception of the objects around us, but they could be wrong. Despite all our experience, it is possible (however bizarre) that we might all be systematically electrochemically stimulated into thinking and experiencing the world as we seem to and yet we are actually in the Matrix or are subject to some other kind of

brain stimulation in a super-lab. Beyond such a radical reply, a
defense of religious experience could underscore the apparent
coherence of reported experiences, their ostensibly public
character, and so on. This, however, brings us to a second worry.

Michael Martin and others have charged that reported
religious experiences are unstable and in conflict.

> Religious experience … tell[s] no uniform or coherent story,
> and there is no plausible theory to account for discrepancies
> among them. Again the situation could be different. Imagine a
> possible world where part of reality can only be known through
> religious experiences. There religious experiences would tend
> to tell a coherent story. Not only would the descriptions of the
> experience be coherent, but the descriptions of the experiences
> of different people would tend to be consistent with one
> another. Indeed, a religious experience in one culture would
> generally corroborate a religious experience in another culture.
> When there was a lack of corroboration, there would be a
> plausible explanation for the discrepancy.

(Martin 1990, 159)

And he offers some of the following as marks of discrepancy:

> In the Western tradition, God is a person distinct from the
> world and from His creatures. Not surprisingly, many religious
> experiences within the Western tradition, especially non-mysti-
> cal ones such as the experience of God speaking to someone
> and giving advice and counsel, convey this idea of God. On the
> other hand, mystical religious experience within the Eastern
> tradition tends to convey a pantheistic and impersonal God.
> The experience of God in this tradition typically is not that of
> a caring, loving person but of an impersonal absolute and
> ultimate reality. To be sure, this difference is not uniform:
> There are theistic trends in Hinduism and pantheistic trends in
> Christianity. But the differences between East and West are

> sufficiently widespread ... and they certainly seem incompatible. A God that transcends the world seemingly cannot be identical with the world; a God that is a person can apparently not be impersonal.
>
> (Martin 1990, 178)

Because neither God nor any object can have contradictory properties, religious experience cannot serve as reliable evidence for theism or other religious hypotheses.

One reply is that we simply do not find the wide conflict posited by Martin and others. As Martin concedes, religious experiences are not so limited to cultures that one cannot find broadly theistic notions of God across many contexts. Arguably a very general form of theism can be found in reported religious experiences in Judaism, Christianity, and Islam, and theistic traditions within Hinduism, Buddhism, African religions, Sikhism, aboriginal or primary religions, Confucianism, and other religions.

Some of the differences Martin cites may also be seen as less radical than they first appear. Martin notes the discrepancy between those who claim to experience a God that is identical with the world and a God that transcends the world. To be sure, there is no middle ground between thinking that God is identical with the world and thinking that God is not identical with the world. But some theologians have articulated a view of God that is at once embodied or immanent as well as transcendent. On this view, insistence upon the transcendence of God secures the conviction that God is more than the material, created cosmos. But it does not follow that God is less than the created cosmos or that the cosmos could not function in some way like a divine embodiment. The difference between God being 'a caring loving person' and 'an impersonal absolute and ultimate reality' may at first also seem a stark, ineliminable difference. But even here the contrast need not be strict. Could God be at once personal and yet also appear to have an impersonal aspect? God might be adequately described as a person insofar as God has intentions, knowledge, and acts, and yet God may be described as impersonal in that God necessarily exists or that as an essentially good being God can function as a moral reference point (via divine laws or principles) and thus appears to be an abstract entity of sorts. In this way, there may be far less conflict between religious experiences than Schellenberg proposes. Someone's experience of God's loving presence may complement an experience of God as an oceanic, awesome unity.

Objection 2: Religious experiences can be accounted for on terms other than positing a transcendent divine power, e.g. hypnotism, the desire for divine assistance, political power by appeal to divine authority, and so on. There are naturalistic accounts of religious experience involving guilt and unconscious urges and projections (Freud), economics (Marx), and resentment (Nietzsche). Any of these seem to provide simpler, more elegant accounts of religious experience than invoking a transcendent, divine reality.

There is no easy way to reply to this charge, for I think that this is where theism and naturalism need to be weighed in terms of cumulative, comprehensive arguments. If some of the earlier theistic arguments have plausibility, that lends weight to the claims of actually experiencing the divine. But if naturalism is well established, then somehow religious experiences need to be explained away.

Evidence and evidentialism

In this and some future chapters the focus is on the evidence for different religious beliefs, but it is worth noting that some philosophers reject what they call *evidentialism*, the thesis that if some belief is warranted it must be based on evidence. Alvin

Plantinga, Nicholas Wolterstorff, and other philosophers have proposed that theistic beliefs may emerge naturally or in accord with a reliable sense of God which is not a matter of reproducible, public evidence. What if persons under a variety of circumstances – from attending religious services to experiencing an awesome natural event – found themselves having beliefs about God's existence and nature?

These philosophers, sometimes grouped together as *reformed epistemologists*, challenge the idea that beliefs in general are only warranted if they are based on evidence. They contend that if the standard for evidence were substantial, very few basic common sense beliefs would be warranted. Even our beliefs that there are other persons and that our ordinary perceptions and memories are reliable seem more instinctual or natural than justified by carefully defended premises and rigorous inferences. Plantinga and others have argued that the philosophical ideal – launched in the Enlightenment by René Descartes and John Locke – that all our beliefs can be rigorously established though incontrovertible evidence is dead. The human condition is, rather, a fallible one in which our standards for appropriate belief and doubt are not always subject to strict standards of evidence. Reformed epistemologists contend that just as our bodily organs have natural functions (the pancreas, liver, and heart can function well or badly) it may be that we are so constituted to naturally believe that there is a God. Our bodily organs do not work on laws of evidence and our religious beliefs may be no worse, since they also do not depend on evidential relations.

In developing and defending this position, reformed epistemologists have devoted themselves to three projects: (I) the critiques of evidentialism; (II) building a case against the thesis that theism is known to be false and that the causes of theistic beliefs are known to be irrational or ignoble (e.g. religious belief is based upon infantile fear); (III) developing an overall theistic worldview that would (if true) account for the naturalness of religious belief.

Reformed epistemology is a substantial movement that faces some challenges. In practice, some of its advocates seem to rely on an implicit evidentialism. Thus, Plantinga has on many occasions reported that his own conviction that there is a God stemmed from religious experience (Plantinga 2008). It also has been objected that the movement is largely a defensive one, for its advocates do not so much argue for the truth of theism as for the position that theistic belief can be warranted even if it is not known to be true.

In the last chapter we will take up what may be called the ethics of belief. When, if ever, can a responsible person with intellectual integrity accept a religious belief (or any belief) on little or no evidence?

4
The problem of evil

Philosophical and religious reflection on the nature of evil is foundational to the history of culture. One of the oldest surviving texts we have, *Gilgamesh*, takes as foundational the problem of suffering and death. All the world religions advance the thesis that our world of suffering and violence is in some sense wrong or bad and out of harmony with what ought to be. Can death be overcome? Is such suffering compatible with an all-powerful, all-knowing, all-good God?

Although in this chapter I am treating the problem of evil in the context of the theistic–naturalist debate, it has been a major point of contention between Hinduism and Buddhism as well. Many of the lines of reasoning employed by theists were developed on the Indian subcontinent by Hindus responding to objections from Buddhist philosophers. For example, accounting for evil by appealing to greater goods and the reality of freedom has been just as important to Hindu philosophers replying to Buddhist critics as it has to theists replying to naturalists.

Some basic values and disvalues

Among the *disvalues* in the cosmos, we can begin with pain. (Some philosophers distinguish pain and suffering: 'pain' referring to physiologically based sensations and 'suffering' referring to hardships that go beyond sensations.) Pain can serve some essential biological need and may be required to achieve something good, as in training for athletics, and perhaps some pains may be justified to achieve some great good, like the pain of a necessary operation. But what about the vast amount of pain that does not seem to serve any possible good? Vast numbers, perhaps the overwhelming majority, of humans (and non-human animals too) suffer pain that serves no evident good. Why all this pain and suffering?

The three monotheistic traditions each affirm that the cosmos is not how it should be. The created order is not in concord with the will and nature of its creator. But now consider the question of whether the concept of God's power and limitless goodness is compatible with God's sustaining of such a cosmos? If God is all-good, all-knowing, and perfectly powerful, why did God create and sustain a cosmos in which so many suffer so greatly? This seems to many to be by itself adequate evidence that God does not exist. Even for those convinced of God's existence, it is not a question to be answered glibly.

Those theists who advance what they believe is a plausible, positive account of the coexistence of evil and the goodness of God are advancing a *theodicy*. A less ambitious task is offering what is technically called a *defense*: a logically possible account of evil in support of the view that evil does not disprove the existence of God. A defense stops short of claiming the plausibility of a theodicy and seeks only to show that the existence and scope of evil do not render theism unreasonable.

There are many replies to the question raised by the problem of evil. One classic answer is the greater good philosophy, according to which the cosmic evils are necessary conditions for greater goods. Without the natural possibility (and virtual certainty) of evil there could not be such great goods as responsible, free, created agents whose lives are interdependent and a realm of action that is in some sense independent of God. Subsequent reflection and argument are then needed to clarify and test the value of these goods (how significant a good is freedom?) and explore whether it is reasonable or not to believe that an all-good God would allow cosmic evil for the sake of such greater goods.

There are still other positions: some argue that evil is not evidence against God's existence at all because we are not in a position to know whether or not the evils of the cosmos serve or make possible greater goods, while others concede that evil *does* constitute evidence against God's existence but the value of the evidence is undermined or even overcome by an independent awareness of the existence of a good God. The second position may be illustrated with a simple analogy. Imagine that a body of evidence (taken alone) makes it highly likely that you robbed a bank (eyewitnesses claim to have seen you, the getaway car matched yours, you suddenly came into a lot of money you couldn't account for, and so on). We should accept the conclusion that you robbed the bank, given that evidence, but as it happens we have evidence that you were out of town at the time (witnesses claim to have seen you) and testimony to your character indicating that you would never rob a bank. We might well believe that you are innocent based on the second set of evidence, while admitting that we had no good way to explain the first. A theist may claim to have independent and sufficient reasons for believing in an all-good God (based on religious experience or the ontological argument, for example) and yet concede that if the only evidence were the scope of cosmic evil they would conclude that God does not exist.

Let us consider a number of arguments for and against the existence of God responding to the problem of evil, including what may be called: the primacy of the good; the nature of freedom; non-human animal suffering; comparing possible worlds; the 'hiddenness of God' objection; the concept of absolute wrong; and the radical difference between considering the goodness of an agent within the cosmos and considering the goodness of one who creates the cosmos.

The primacy of the good

One important theistic line of reasoning, used in providing both a theodicy and a defense, has been to argue that the goodness of the cosmos is more fundamental than the evil. This is sometimes called the *privati boni* (the privation of good) thesis. It may at first glance seem profoundly implausible, but it argues that the evil of evil acts depends upon the fact that people and animals are good. Harming or killing a person involves the breaking down or terminating of a good life. Goodness is antecedent to evil; without goodness there would be no evil.

Is this thesis plausible? It has some credibility. If 'good' or 'goodness' is defined in a sufficiently broad fashion, it is hard to see how there might be evil without good. Imagine a gunman resolved to kill the innocent. Unless he possesses some 'goods' (the good of thought, memory, motion, skill, passion, and physical coordination) he would not be able to do any substantially evil acts. And unless those he is shooting also possess some 'goods' or are themselves good no evil would occur.

In the fifth century, Augustine defended the *privati boni* thesis with the following thought experiment. He asks his readers to imagine the worst possible creature, Cacus, 'so unsociable and savage that they perhaps preferred to call him a semi-human rather than a human being', a being 'unequalled in wickedness'. Augustine contends that even such a horrific monster must still be conceived of in terms of basic goods (the desire for bodily integrity, an inner peace of sorts) underlying all the savagery (Augustine 1972 [426], XIX, 12).

Without the good of bodily integrity (motor control, the capacity to think, feel, sense), Cacus would not survive to be wicked. One might argue that thinking and feeling are activities that lack inherent value, but the powers to think and feel seem to be central powers of a healthy human person. If someone reported that a fellow human being had lost the power of thought, sensation, the ability to move, and so on, we would not need to ask whether this was bad for the person.

But what about a contrary, 'privation of evil' principle? Might it be the case that goodness is just the breaking down of evil or the absence of evil? We might well understand health (in part) as the absence of disease, but that would be a very weak concept of health and only as helpful as describing someone with hair as having an absence of baldness. Moreover, some goods seem to require evil. Arguably, a person courageously rescuing an innocent person from a wicked assailant is good and yet it is only good, ceteris paribus, if there actually *is* a threatening, wicked assailant.

Even if we accept the *privati boni* thesis, by itself it will not relieve the problem of evil. Perhaps there could not be evil without good, but why so much evil? And couldn't there be a great deal of good without evil? Replying to these questions frequently focuses on the nature and value of freedom. Some argue that for persons to be morally and religiously responsible for others and for the world (a great good), there must be at least the possibility, if not the extreme likelihood, of evil.

The nature of freedom

According to what is called the *free will defense*, one cannot rule out the goodness of God because it is possible that the origin of evil, or much evil, stems from free agents. While the appeal to freedom often takes place in a defense, it is also frequently used in theodicies. Some philosophers claim that free agency is itself a basic, fundamental good. In other words freedom should be valued for itself, not because it generates some other good. There is some reason to think that many of us assume such a view. If you were freely walking under ordinary conditions and someone shouted out to you, 'STOP!' you would probably be quite put out if the person had no reason whatever for issuing such a command (perhaps they were playing a game). Other things being equal, I suggest we do take the capacity to move and make deliberate choices as a basic good. The intuitive plausibility of this judgment may be enhanced if we imagine that a stranger did not simply yell, 'STOP!' but forcibly and without your permission restrained you from walking your intended walk. They then frogmarched you by way of another route as they had – correctly – judged that the latter route was a quicker one for you to take to arrive at the destination that they knew you wanted to get to. Even though you would then have got to where you wanted to get to more quickly than had you been allowed freely to go your own way, you would still have something to complain about. And a good reason behind this complaint is the inherent goodness of freedom.

Consider, however, the following objection. Imagine you are freely engaged in some wrong such as breaking a promise. Would the fact that you were freely breaking the promise affect our evaluation of the act? If freedom is a basic good, should we conclude that while the act was wrong, the fact that you did so freely was at least some sign of value? In other words, does the inherent goodness that some philosophers attribute to freedom help make your freely chosen wrongful act a little less wrong, simply because it was committed freely? If anything, it seems one would judge the act more severely, rather than less, if it were done freely. If you had been compelled to break the promise, for example, we might readily excuse the promise-breaking or even question whether you actually broke a promise. (If you were compelled to miss an appointment by a gunman, I doubt anyone would say you were in a position to make or break the earlier promise.)

The above examples do not obviously undermine the intrinsic goodness of freedom. Arguably, in order to do some act that truly deserves moral censure, you have to possess a certain power: the power to exercise judgment freely and reflectively. Infants and the severely handicapped are not considered moral agents (deserving of blame or praise for their moral virtues) largely because they lack the value of reflective freedom. If, however, the above objection still gives one pause about whether freedom is a basic good, it is still plausible to think that some goods involve the freedom whether to act or not. If you are to care for the welfare of another person freely, don't you have to be free not to? There appear to be many states (for example, persons freely loving each other) that are intrinsically good that require freedom, and this freedom seems to be good, regardless of whether it is valuable for its own sake. Now we come to two accounts of the nature of freedom: libertarian free will, and compatabilism.

According to *libertarian free will*, you freely engaged in the care of another person when you did so and had the power not to do so. Such libertarian freedom is intuitively appealing and in line with much common sense. It may not be the *only* form of freedom, however. According to one form of what is called *compatabilism*, you freely do X if you do X, you wanted to do X (and possibly you even wanted to want to do X), you were not controlled by external intelligent forces (no hypnosis), and you would not have done X if you had different desires. Such an account is impressive, but it may not go far enough when thinking about human agents in moral states of affairs. Consider two cases where a subject does X under libertarian conditions and then under compatabilist conditions. In the first, the action is truly *up to them*; it was within their power not to do X. But in the second case the act stemmed from what they wanted, but *they had no power to do otherwise*. Their act was determined by factors beyond themself as an agent, even if there were no hypnotism or the like. If all of your deliberations are fixed and determined by forces outside of yourself as well as by your own body running in accord with exceptionless laws of nature, it is hard to see that you are morally accountable for what you do. There are philosophers who believe we should act as we currently do and praise each other for good acts and blame each other for wrongdoing, even though we have no power to do otherwise. Yet, the justification for continuing this practice would seem to be about social control and safety, rather than authentic praise or blame for something a person did when it was fully up to them.

Arguably, then, libertarian freedom is good; it may or may not be a *basic* good, but so long as it is a constitutive part of good states of affairs it seems good. Now let us consider whether it is plausible to think we actually have such freedom.

Determinism is the view that all events that occur do so necessarily, given all antecedent and contemporary conditions and the prevailing laws of nature. It seems that science, for instance, has *not* as yet shown libertarian freedom to be illusory. We currently recognize in quantum mechanics a fundamental indeterminacy in the universe and, though the (alleged) fact of indeterminacy does not by itself establish freedom, it at least prevents one claiming that all science is deterministic. Our best science today seems to function well with probabilistic laws, according to which there may be a sixty per cent chance (but not a certainty) that a photon goes through a slot or a forty per cent chance of atomic decay, and so on. The theory of determinism is extraordinarily ambitious and only requires one counter-example. That is, if determinism is true then no event anywhere in the whole cosmos or any time in the past or future is not necessary (or: each event *is* necessary), given the other events and the laws of nature. On this view, all events are *fixed* and not merely probable or random. Unless determinism is self-evident, it seems we should at least be open to the possibility of libertarian freedom.

The arena in which libertarian freedom makes the most sense

is in a humanistic form of psychology that recognizes teleological or purposive explanations. In this framework, explanations of our actions are in terms of reasons that incline (i.e. are more probable) but without necessitating certain acts. A person does x for reason r, but they might not have done so for reason s. Some have claimed that our experience does not give us evidence of agency. Consider the claim that the experience of freedom is simply a sense that our choices are not compelled. When you freely purchased a computer you felt free because, apart from (apparently) not being hypnotized or threatened, you simply did not feel forced. This is of no value as evidence against determinism, however, since you largely act in ignorance of the causal mechanisms in play. Look back on the purchase and you may conclude that getting the computer was virtually inevitable, given all the surrounding circumstances (Blanshard 1958, 5–6). But this seems to be an implausible account of the experience of agency (Bertocci 1970, 101). The experience of free agency feels like something *we do* as opposed to something *that happens to us*. Thinking about what act to do appears to be something we undertake like running rather than a passive occurrence like being pushed or suddenly feeling a headache or indigestion. Our experience of agency seems to be based, not on ignorance, but on a felt power to do or refrain from doing some act.

Consider just one more argument against libertarian freedom: If you freely elect to do X rather than not-X, *why* did you do so? This question need not be mysterious. Imagine you decided to give to charity rather than buy coffee because of a recent conversation with a friend engaged in famine relief. Why did *that* conversation sway you? Don't we have to appeal to your character, your dispositions, and so on? Unless you can claim to have created your character and dispositions, shouldn't we reject libertarian freedom and conclude instead that the act was determined by your character and dispositions? This argument seeks to overturn the notion that responsibility requires liberation agency. Perhaps, rather, if we are truly responsible for our actions we need to adopt a form of determinism: responsible action is determined by our characters.

This line of reasoning has weight, but what it largely draws attention to is that if we truly are free in morally relevant conditions, then we must be responsible for our character and dispositions. We do not develop a character in one big act of freedom (or, at least, this would seem to be rare), but one may plausibly hold that one's character is built up slowly through indefinitely many decisions when it was *up to you* how you acted. Does this involve a mysterious type of self-transcendence or self-causing? Hardly – it may only involve you entertaining two states of affairs: one in which you are generous and charitable, and one in which you are not. By giving to charity you make it the case that the one state of affairs (of the charitable character) is *yours*. In the absence of a powerful reason for thinking otherwise, libertarian freedom seems plausible. Libertarian agency may appear to be a mystery if one assumes there can only be either deterministic explanations or brute random happenings. But to anyone who has reflected carefully on the process of deliberation this seems to leave out a third option: persons can themselves weigh reasons and decide to act on some reasons rather than others.

If we grant for the sake of argument that there is valuable libertarian free agency, is theism secure? Not quite. A great deal of evil may be through freely willed malice, and it may be that many natural disasters would be less terrible if persons used their freedom more compassionately. But consider whether free agency is worth all the evil that exists. And what of the evils that stem from non-free agents like the evils that occur in non-human animal suffering? Let's look at animal suffering and then return to the appeal to freedom and other goods.

Non-human animal suffering

How are we to understand the apparent suffering in the non-human animal world? This is a world of suffering that extends well beyond matters of free agency. There is one radical possibility I note simply to set aside. There are philosophers who deny that there is such suffering. Some argue that, though there is pain behavior, shrieks, controlled action to avoid pain, and so on, most non-human animals lack the neural organic base to suffer. Non-human animals, on this view, only have ways to sense or record injury. This sensory capacity – *nociception* – leads organisms to avoid or minimize injury. A leech or slug, for example, has nociception. But in many organisms (especially non-vertebrates) there seems to be insufficient brain capacity to collate and ground an experience of pain. With vertebrates we have evidence of brain processes that are integral to injury-avoiding behavior, but we see great differences among different animals in the role of the brain in such behavior. Some scientists and philosophers have argued that it is only when you have primates and humans with a developed neocortex that you have grounds for recognizing suffering and morally relevant pain.

The case against animal suffering is developed both in terms of neurology and through the use of Ockham's razor. Some have argued that if there are no compelling reasons to posit non-human animal suffering, we should not do so.

I think the above reasoning should give us pause in claiming we *know* the extent of non-human suffering (we should resist a simple anthropomorphizing of animals), but it is too extreme in its diminished view of animal suffering. Although it is possible for there to be intelligent behavior without full consciousness – people sleepwalk – it is implausible to think of the rest of the animal world as, in effect, sleepwalkers. Rather than adopt such a severe view or worse (e.g. assume non-human animals are akin to automata as in Disney's 'Hall of Presidents'), let us acknowledge non-human animal pain and suffering.

The best-known case for atheism based on apparent evil was developed by William Rowe and involved animal suffering. Rowe argued that there exists intense suffering that an omnipotent being could have prevented without losing a great good or causing a greater harm. If that being is wholly good, the harm would have been prevented. Hence there is no wholly good, omnipotent being. Rowe offered the following case of preventable harm:

> Suppose in some distant forest lightning strikes a dead tree, resulting in a forest fire. In the fire a fawn is trapped, horribly burned, and lies in terrible agony for several days before death relieves its suffering. So far as we can see, the fawn's intense suffering is pointless. For there does not appear to be any greater good such that the prevention of the fawn's suffering would require either the loss of that good or the occurrence of an evil equally bad or worse. Nor does there seem to be any equally bad or worse evil so connected to the fawn's suffering that it would have had to occur had the fawn's suffering been prevented. Could an omnipotent, omniscient being have prevented the fawn's apparently pointless suffering? The answer is obvious, as even the theist will insist. An omnipotent, omniscient being could have easily prevented the fawn from being horribly burned, or, given the burning, could have spared the fawn the intense suffering by quickly ending its life, rather than allowing the fawn to lie in terrible agony for several days.

(Rowe 2003, 370)

Rowe holds that in the absence of evidence that some good was achieved by the fawn's suffering or that the suffering was the consequence of some good (or the avoidance of some evident evil), it is rational to conclude there is no wholly good, omnipotent god.

How might a theist reply? Probably the most promising approach would be ecological. Most contemporary ecologists (and most environmentalists) place greater emphasis on the well-being of species rather than of individuals such as Rowe's fawn. Consider this extensive reflection on natural evil by the ecological philosopher Holmes Rolston III:

> Nature is random, contingent, blind, disastrous, wasteful, indifferent, selfish, cruel, clumsy, ugly, struggling, full of suffering, and, ultimately, death? Yes, but this sees only the shadows, and there has to be light to cast shadows. Nature is orderly, prolific, efficient, selecting for adapted fit, exuberant, complex, diverse, regenerating life generation after generation. There are disvalues in nature as surely as there are values, and the disvalues systemically drive the value achievements. Translated into theological terms, the evils are redeemed in the ongoing story.
>
> Look, for instance, at predation. Certainly from the perspective of any particular animal as prey, being eaten is a bad thing. But then again the disvalue to the prey is a value to the predator, and, further, with a systemic turn, perspectives change. There is not value loss so much as value capture; there is appropriation of nutrient materials and energy from one life stream to another, with selective pressures to be efficient about the transfer. The pains of the prey are redeemed, we might say, by the pleasures of the predator. There are many biological achievements in muscle, power, sentience, and intelligence that could only have evolved, at least in life as we know it on Earth, with predation.
>
> Could, should God have created a world with only flora, no fauna? Possibly. Possibly not, since in a world in which things are assembled something has to disassemble them for recycling.

In any case, we do not think that a mere floral world would be of more value than a world with fauna also. In a mere floral world, there would be no one to think. Heterotrophs must be built on autotrophs, and no autotrophs are sentient or cerebral. Could we have had only plant-eating fauna, only grazers, no predators? Possibly, though probably we never did, since predation preceded photosynthesis. Even grazers are predators of a kind, though what they eat does not suffer. Again, an Earth with only herbivores and no omnivores or carnivores would be impoverished – the animal skills demanded would be only a fraction of those that have resulted in actual zoology – no horns, no fleet-footed predators or prey, no fine-tuned eyesight and hearing, no quick neural capacity, no advanced brains. We humans stand in this tradition, as our ancestors were hunters. We really cannot envision a world, on any Earth more or less like our own, which can give birth to the myriad forms of life that have been generated here, without some things eating other things.

(Rolston 2003, 534)

Rowe's philosophy of animal suffering paints a very different picture. Assuming the fawn is suffering, and that if an agent could prevent such suffering they should do so (assuming there is no other, more stringent obligation), then it seems you and I have an obligation to engage in a radical interference in natural processes. Rowe's view of non-human animals seems to require that those who are able to should rescue fawns from suffering, whether this be from lightning and fire or predation. But for Rolston predation and other natural causes of suffering are part of an overall good ecosystem.

If one were to successfully argue that God can only create a world such as ours if all undeserved suffering be prevented (suffering may be said to be undeserved when it is not merited, as in punishment, and is not for the good of the one who suffers), one would be led to conclude that God should continuously engage in miraculous interventions. Peter van Inwagen suggests that an alternative world of little or no suffering would amount to a virtual absurdity.

> God, by means of a continuous series of ubiquitous miracles, causes a planet inhabited by the same animal life as the actual earth to be a hedonic utopia. On this planet, fawns are (like Shadrach, Meshach, and Abednego) saved by angels when they are in danger of being burnt alive. Harmful parasites and microorganisms suffer immediate supernatural dissolution if they enter a higher animal's body. Lambs are miraculously hidden from lions, and the lions are compensated for the resulting restriction on their diets by physically impossible falls of high-protein manna.
>
> (van Inwagen 2003, 395)

Van Inwagen argues that an evolving biological world such as our own, not subject to continuous divine interference, is compatible with the goodness of God. This investigation into degrees of suffering leads naturally into the whole question of quantifying values.

Comparing possible worlds

The atheist who defends their position by appealing to the magnitude of evil may be initiating a curious form of argument. How much evil is too much? Some philosophers have insisted that an all-good God would not permit *any* undeserved pain or suffering at all. This (in my view) seems too severe a condition. Arguably it is good for there to be a cosmos where there are free creatures dependent upon each other for their welfare and they are able to act in some independence of the power of God. This thesis will be one to question later, but note that a philosopher like Peter van Inwagen seems right that preventing *all* undeserved suffering would not only rule out evolution; it would require God to continuously, miraculously interfere in the natural world. Such continuous divine action would seem to undermine the extent to which one could recognize the cosmos as a stable order of reality. But if the atheist that insists an all-good God should prevent evil, how much evil should God prevent? At this point we seem to have difficulty in assessing the overall goodness or value of worlds.

But, however this is resolved, I think the theist has a plausible line of argument to the effect that the concept of *a best possible world* is problematic. Imagine any world you like: for instance, indefinitely many happy people with abundant goods. There may be a problem with the very concept of such a world if the people have libertarian agency, for if there is bona fide freedom even God cannot guarantee such a happy outcome (assuming that omniscience does not include perfect knowledge of future free acts). But, more fundamentally, given any world we imagine, it seems as though we can conceive of a better world simply by adding one additional happy person. In short, the concept of a best possible world seems like the concept of a greatest possible number. There simply cannot be such a number, for every integer has a greater integer.

Consider one objection to the argument that there can be no best possible world. A world in which there are one hundred happy people does not seem worse than a world in which everything is the same but there is one more person as happy as each of the hundred in the first. Goodness of worlds is not additive in the way that people are. A world with any number of people each of whom was perfectly happy, content, free, and so on (fill in as many good-making features as you like) would be equally good as any world in which there were any other number of people in this state. In this framework there may not be one best possible world, for there could be lots of equally good worlds. The question for the theist may be reformulated from 'Why didn't God create the best possible world?' to 'Why didn't God create one of these equally good worlds?'

This is a forceful reply, but I suggest goodness is additive, just as evil is additive. Obviously, we do not routinely make judgments about what kind of worlds to make, but when we do make decisions about the distribution of goods or harms we do give weight to numbers. If we are choosing between two economic policies that provide benefits to either ten percent or a hundred per cent of the population, ceteris paribus, the larger distribution of benefits seems to be a positive value. Similarly with hardship: a world in which a hundred people endure undeserved suffering seems worse than one in which 6.8 billion people endure such suffering. From a moral point of view we may think someone who murders one person is equally evil (blameworthy) as a serial murderer and deserves equal punishment. But this should not eclipse the notion that the serial murderer has produced a greater horror, affecting more people. Arguably, one *can* treat worlds as better or worse depending upon numbers, and so the case against the very idea of a best possible world remains plausible.

In addition to the categories of theistic replies to the problem of evil, atheist arguments usually fall into two broad categories. According to advocates of the *logical problem of evil*, it can be established that the existence of *any evil at all* is incompatible with the goodness of God. Although this line of reasoning has contemporary defenders, the more popular charge is called the *evidential problem of evil*, according to which some evil is compatible with God's goodness, but not the magnitude of evil that is evident. Stanley Kane allows that some evil may be essential for some goods (e.g. developing a moral character), but he argues that a desirable good end may be achieved with less suffering.

Courage and fortitude, for instance, could manifest themselves as the persistence, steadfastness, and perseverance it takes to accomplish well any difficult or demanding long-range task – the writing of a doctoral dissertation, for example, or training for and competing in the Olympic Games. ... It is hard to see why a man or a woman cannot develop just as much patience, fortitude and strength of character in helping his or her spouse complete a doctoral dissertation as in caring for a sick child through a long and serious illness.

(Kane 1975, 2f)

Kane may be right and great goods might be made possible or actual with less evil. On the other hand, William Hasker has argued that a cosmos with internal integrity and real independence of God cannot rule out gratuitous evils:

It is *good* that there be such a creation, endowed as it is with enormous potentialities for the enrichment of life and existence. The relative autonomy allowed both to human beings and to nature means, however, that the good endowments of the creation are open also to the possibility of the events and actions we identify as evil ... A world in which this was not so – a world in which creatures either lack powers of their own or in which God constantly intervenes to prevent those powers from acting in ways that are less than optimal – would be a world without internal integrity; the existence of such a world would add little of worth over and above the value of God's simply imagining it. God, however, has instead chosen a creation that is *really there* – that has a genuine integrity and autonomy of its own. And it is good that this is so.

(Hasker 2008, 201–2)

How are we to assess the ostensibly possible world that Kane describes versus the actual world that Hasker proposes is good notwithstanding the magnitude of evil?

I do not think it is an easy task to contrast possible worlds and correspondingly assign some precise boundary of suffering compatible or incompatible with God's goodness. Partly this is because if it is a good thing for creatures to have profound responsibility for each other, it is difficult to set a limit on how creatures might behave. A world in which my responsibility for myself and others is limited to training for the Olympics, or assisting a graduate student in their dissertation, seems a world in which there is very little *deep responsibility*. And once one allows for free, interdependent responsibility and a stable world without regular miracles, it seems hard to determine when God should step in and rupture human history. At this juncture it is important to consider a new move in the literature about the problem of evil. Shouldn't an all-good God actually make it easier for us to tell whether the creation is good and upheld by a good creator?

The hiddenness of God objection

Some of the arguments we have been considering – Rowe's, for example – seem to hold that if some evil occurs and there is an all-good God, then we would know why God permitted the evil. Rowe allows that it may be reasonable to still believe in an all-good God without knowing why evil occurs if our evidence for God rests on good, independent grounds. This is illustrated by the case of identifying the bank robber. Still, Rowe thinks, and John Schellenberg has recently argued, an all-good God would not leave us in the dark about why there is evil. Schellenberg develops the following thought experiment.

Imagine you are playing hide and seek with your mother. You have been hiding from her but then desire to see her. She is nowhere to be found. You call out for her. You think you hear her but it is only the sound of the wind. 'Would your mother – loving and responsible parent that she is – fail to answer if she were around?' (Schellenberg 2007, 228) Schellenberg thinks God's not answering an honest call for divine revelation is evidence that God does not exist. Schellenberg offers another thought experiment. Suppose your daughter has a distorted view of you that prevents her having a good, fulfilling relationship with you. Wouldn't you do almost *anything* to expose this distortion and facilitate a healthy parent–child relationship?

> Now suppose that some way of instantaneously transforming her perspective is made available to you: if you press this button she will see you for who you really are and all the snagged and tangled and distorted beliefs will rearrange themselves into a clear perception of the truth. Surely you will use this means of cutting through that mess, for it represents only an abbreviated version of what you have already been seeking.
>
> (Schellenberg 2007, 224–5)

Because we live in a world where people persist in disbelieving God or having cruel views of God, and God does not appear to correct these states, it is evident that God does not exist.

A theist may introduce various replies. One is that the parables are incomplete. Most religious, theistic traditions hold that there is an afterlife (a topic in the next chapter) and so there will be a time when the 'daughter' and 'child' will be reunited with the parent-God. To address this broader theistic perspective, Schellenberg would need a premise like: An all-good God would never allow a creature to seek God without finding God in an evident fashion. The problem with justifying this premise is that one would need to rule out great goods that may be available from being a non-theist in a world in which theism is correct and God does exist and we are part of God's creation. Schellenberg's parables may be effective insofar as we imagine human parents, but when one thinks about a creator from a theistic point of view one is considering whether a creator would value humans (and perhaps other creatures) living independently of divine guidance. Wouldn't a cosmos in which every time you doubted God you heard a voice though the leaves and wind assuring you of God's presence be one in which you are essentially being treated like an infant?

The second parable also raises questions about manipulation and control. Imagine your daughter truly is estranged from you. Yes, you might try to convince her of your goodness, but the idea of pushing a button to transform her seems open to charges of manipulation. It also eclipses another consideration: your daughter's false view of you might lead her to do great things. Let's change the parable slightly. Imagine your daughter wrongly believes you are a narcissistic miser who has had a major role in arms sales to rogue nations. Imagine also that, at some distant point in the future, she will know the truth about your good character and love for her. In the meantime imagine she has (in open revolt against what she thinks of you) developed a selfless love for others that leads her to make an effective contribution to world peace and a non-violent planet. Would you press the button then?

Schellenberg might concede that under *those* conditions one should not push the button, but in reality few people who are unaware of God's reality are in that position. Schellenberg seems to hold that all (or virtually all) seekers of the divine would find fulfillment in relation to God, and that if God is all-good, God would bring about such a relationship.

Schellenberg may be right, but there is reason to believe he needs a stronger and more difficult-to-establish thesis. Granted (for the sake of argument) all of what Schellenberg claims about the goodness of a relationship with God, and granted an all-good God will enable such a relationship, does it convincingly follow that God would enable that relationship at every time in a person's life? Given the possibility of an afterlife, it may be that the divine–human relationship will take place for many of us beyond this life. (We will address the possibility of an afterlife in the next chapter.)

The debate over God's so-called hiddenness connects up with a recent movement in philosophy of religion called *skeptical theism*. These theists are skeptical about any claims to know the goods that may justify God's creating or conserving the cosmos, but they contend that we should not expect to know such justificatory goods. If we should not expect to be able to make such a finding, then a failure to grasp why such ills occur is not sufficient to infer that there are no good reasons that God may have for permitting evil. Marilyn Adams's recent work on evil proposes that there may be great goods that are much greater than any goods we may currently conceive and that these goods may overcome the evils in the cosmos. God's reasons for sustaining a creation that involves horrendous evil may be ones we are currently unable to fathom; we may be cognitively, emotionally, and/or spiritually too immature to grasp such reasons 'the way a two-year-old child is incapable of understanding its mother's reasons for permitting surgery' (Adams 1999, 216–17).

Absolute wrongs

Let's consider a different line of reasoning. Might it be the case that there are some cosmic evils that no reason of any kind might permit an all-good God to allow? The Holocaust and the rape and murder of children might count as *absolute wrongs*. Given absolute wrongs, we may conclude there is no all-good, all-powerful, all-knowing God. This line of reasoning might even raise a sinister side to theism: If such horrors as genocide and rape are actually justified, should we regret their occurrence?

After all, if God is justified in allowing great evil for the sake of great goods, shouldn't we do so as well? There are at least four observations to consider in reply.

First, theistic religious tradition treats cosmic evil as a profound violation of God's purpose and nature. From a theistic perspective world evils, far from bring willed by God, are against the core purpose of the cosmos. A question of why God should allow cosmic wrong therefore needs to be articulated as follows if the question is to genuinely bear on theism: why would God not prevent that which profoundly violates God's own nature and will?

Second, many theists today believe that God is affectively responsive to the values of creation. In this view (called *passibilism*), God sorrows over evils in creation and, perhaps too, God is enraged at injustice (as suggested in some biblical verses) and not a passionless, detached spectator. The problem of evil, therefore, needs yet more expansion: why would God not prevent that which profoundly violates God's own nature and will and is the source of divine sorrow and rage?

Third, there is an important distinction to be made between justification and redemption. Many theists (if not virtually all) hold that world evils are *not* justified. The Holocaust ought not to have happened, regardless of whether it contributed to some good (e.g. the founding of the state of Israel) or not. Theistic tradition focuses mainly on redemption: is it possible for God to bring some healing, reform, or regeneration out of an evil state of affairs? The importance of this question will be vital to the next chapter. Here I simply register the point that in theistic responses to evil there is a major difference between an all-good God allowing evil (or not destroying evil persons) in order to bring about redemption, and God allowing evil because this is justified or somehow good. Although traditional theism holds that God is not evil in creating a cosmos containing evil (and thus God is justified in creating and sustaining the cosmos that exists), it is also held that this evil is not itself justified. No creature's free act of evil is ever justified.

Fourth, any assessment of the problem of evil needs to take stock of an overall theistic position that takes into account theistic claims about God's confrontation with evil, and the possibilities for redemption through omnipotent love. Our view of absolute wrongs may be governed by a framework of human action and contexts. Is there a broader setting in which to assess 'absolute wrongs'?

The ethics of creature and creator

The logic behind many versions of the atheistic argument from evil (whether in the logical or evidential format) often equates the ethics of God, or a creator, and the ethics of a creature. Consider the following: If you had the knowledge and power to prevent X (rape and murder, say) and did not do so, would you be unethical? Absent some amazing additional premises (e.g. preventing X would create even more awful evil), most would answer 'yes'. But in the case of assessing the creator, the question needs to be put more broadly. I offer the following larger question with the inclusion of topics we will take up in the next chapter (miracles, incarnation, an afterlife, redemption). Assessing the theistic problem of evil should include raising a question like this:

Is it compatible with the goodness of God to create and sustain a cosmos of great goods – a cosmos with the goods of life, stable laws of nature, the emergence of consciousness, and creatures with powers of sensation, movement, emotions, and thoughts who have moral and religious experiences? The emergence of animal and human life in this cosmos takes place by means of evolution involving massive numbers of births and deaths and suffering caused by disease and predation. Great evils besiege human life, some of which are the result of liberation free will, and other evils emerge from causes with no free agency. The evils of the cosmos are a source of divine sorrow and rage as God works to bring about great good through periods of profound evil (including the Holocaust). In this cosmos, God acts to confront evil through prophets, an incarnation with miracles, and God seeks the redemption of all creatures including victims and victimizers in this life and an afterlife. Some persons believe they encounter the goodness of God in religious experience, but some do not despite their earnest search for a relationship with God. The cosmic evil that occurs is profoundly contrary to God's nature and in violation of God's purpose for the creation.

Some of these elements (incarnation, miracles, and an afterlife) will be addressed in the next chapter. Filling out such a broader framework is essential for a comprehensive assessment of theism in the context of evil. This broader framework allows one also to take up a further theistic approach, which is to argue that theism is in a better (or no worse) position than naturalism in accounting for evil. C. Stephen Langman takes the stance that theism is in no worse a position than its chief rival, naturalism. A theism that advances libertarian freedom is at least able to understand horrendous evils as violating the purpose and nature of the creation, whereas a naturalism that embraces determinism sees all evil as necessary and fixed, given all other events and the laws of nature.

Before turning to broader perspective on good and evil, consider briefly two different theistic approaches to evil. In twentieth-century philosophy of religion a significant range of theists – often called *panentheists* or *process theologians* – have proposed that God is *not* omnipotent. Alfred North Whitehead, Charles Hartshorne, and others have developed rich alternatives to traditional theism which preserve God's goodness or greatness while contending that God is not able to overcome all cosmic evils. On this model, God and creatures are seen as themselves called to confront evil. A second proposal has been to argue that the God of Judaism, Christianity, and Islam is best not seen as a moral agent. The above question about God's goodness seems to be so structured that God as creator can be moral or immoral. Is that structure problematic?

In all the literature referenced till now in this chapter, it is assumed that if there is a God, God is a moral agent. This, however, is worth questioning. Anthony Kenny writes,

> Morality presupposes a moral community: and a moral community must be of beings with a common language, roughly equal powers, and roughly similar needs, desires, and interests. God can no more be part of a moral community with them than he can be part of a political community with them. As Aristotle said, we cannot attribute moral virtues to divinity: the praise would be vulgar. Equally, moral blame would be laughable.
>
> (Kenny 1992, 87)

Brian Davies is the most prominent defender of the same thesis. Davies holds that God is good but he denies this is the good of moral agency.

> [S]hould we allow ourselves to get caught up in debates about God's moral integrity? A reason for doing so is that many people assume that 'God is good' means 'God is morally good.' Many others, however, do not assume this. Such people, I should stress, are not denying that God is good. Nor are they suggesting that God is immoral. Their position, rather, is that it is wrong to think of God as something either moral (well behaved) or immoral (badly behaved). Their idea is that, whether we are theists or non-theists, there are grounds for

resisting claims like 'God is a good moral agent' or 'God is morally praiseworthy.' And there is a lot to be said for that line of thinking.

(Davies 2006, 227)

Has Davies effectively pointed out how theism can side-step the problem of evil?

Davies's proposal rightly highlights that an assessment of the goodness of God is not on the same level as humans assessing each other, or even weighing the ostensible moral behavior of some non-human animals (can there be an incident where one ape murders another?). Davies will probably need some kind of *privati boni* thesis according to which God has authored a good creation, thereby casting evil as that which is not so much created but as that which corrodes and breaks down creation. Even with that additional move, however, Davies's theism still faces questions about why there are such profound anti-creation forces in the cosmos. There still seems to be a need to consider possibilities of how evil might be defeated or redemption occur, whether or not God is considered a moral agent. Davies's theism also appears to be in some tension with religious traditions in which God appears to act as a moral agent (the biblical God makes promises, welcomes a covenant with people of faith, God is said to love justice, and so on).

The natural next step is to consider the parameter of possible divine agency. Is it possible or reasonable to think there is life after death?

5

Divine action: miracles, the afterlife, and redemption

Is physical death the annihilation of the human person, or is some kind of afterlife possible or desirable? In this chapter let us consider several related topics dealing with the nature of divine action. We begin with the possibility and value of an afterlife, and then, as most (but not all) beliefs in an afterlife involve divine action, the topic of miracles. Some philosophers have pursued the problem of evil into the next life, arguing against the existence of God on the grounds that it is evil for God to damn persons or condemn persons to hell; this requires an exploration of the concepts of redemption and salvation. One possible theistic response to the problem of evil is to argue that God will bring about universal salvation for all; this raises questions about the relationship between religions, particularly whether different religions could be different but equally valid paths to the sacred or the divine.

Is life after death possible?

One reason for thinking the answer must be 'no' is that human persons are not just embodied beings (persons *having* bodies) but *are* bodies. If our bodies are destroyed, we are destroyed. After all, if you *are* your body, then whatever happens to your body happens to you. The most radical response to this position is to argue that such a materialist position is mistaken. Let us therefore consider whether an alternative to materialism is credible; but before doing so let us take seriously the idea that there might be an afterlife even if it turns out we are thoroughly material beings.

One of the more unusual developments in the contemporary philosophy of religion is the number of Christian philosophers who subscribe to some form of materialism and yet hold that there is an afterlife. Peter van Inwagen, Lynne Baker, Trenton Merricks, Bruce Reichenbach, and Kevin Corcoran all hold that while God is a non-physical purposive being, we are exclusively physical. Traditionally, Christians have tended to believe in the soul as an immaterial center of personal identity, though there are notable exceptions (Tertullian and Thomas Hobbes) and Thomas Aquinas affirmed the unity of soul and body in this life. In any case, some contemporary Christian philosophers believe that a materialist view of persons is better able to account for the Christian view that the death of persons is bad and the incarnation of God as an embodied being is good. Let us consider their positive case for an afterlife.

Christian materialists tend to adopt one of four models for an afterlife: resurrection, replication, recreation, and reconstitution.

The resurrection model

On this model (which seems anchored in the New Testament), a person's body may dissolve and, from our vantage point, become scattered through time and space. Parts of one's body may even become parts of other bodies. It still remains possible, if there is an omnipotent God, that the core identity of one's body might again be brought together at a later time (the resurrection) to constitute the person.

This does not seem impossible. The disassembly and reassembly of material objects seems straightforward. Trenton Merricks comments on this option with an example:

Consider ... a watch that is disassembled, perhaps for cleaning. Suppose that, as a result, it ceases to exist. Suppose further that when its parts are reassembled, that watch comes back into existence. The watch thus traverses a temporal gap. Of course, the watch example is controversial. But the claim that the watch jumps through time via disassembly and reassembly – even if it makes questionable assumptions here and there – is at least coherent. It is not contradictory or obviously absurd. It is not, for example, like the claim that one has found a round square in one's pocket, next to the number seven.

(Merricks 2001, 184–5)

The resurrection model may be vexed by a question about just what parts of your body are essential to identity. God might use parts of you to 'resurrect' what appears to be you, but what if God were to make three of you out of your bodily parts? Would there be just one 'real you' and two replicas? If so, which two would be the replicas? These questions may not reveal insuperable difficulties, but they invite some alternative models.

The replica model

Though some worry about the possibility of replication confusing personal identity, some philosophers seem to think replication is promising. John Hick introduces his speculative account of an afterlife by describing someone who disappears from a gathering in London and instantly appears at a similar gathering in New York:

The person who appears in New York is exactly similar, as to both bodily and mental characteristics, to the person who disappears in London. There is continuity of memory, complete similarity of bodily features, including fingerprints, hair and eye coloration and stomach contents, and also of beliefs, habits and mental propensities. In fact there is everything that would lead

us to identify the one who appeared with the one who disap-
peared, except continuous occupancy of space.

(Hick 1978, 280)

He then changes the thought experiment to involve the death
of the person in London and the person's reappearance in New
York as a 'replica' (Hick 1978, 284).

Hick may be right that under these conditions we would
identify the person in New York as the same person who died,
but there remains the problem that personal identity seems to
involve more than replication. Brian Davies presents a forceful
challenge by imagining that you have poisoned the person in
London.

> But, you say: 'Don't worry. I've arranged for a replica of you
> to appear. The replica will seem to have all your memories. He
> will be convinced that he is you. And he will look exactly like
> you. He will even have your fingerprints.' Should I be relieved?
> Speaking for myself, I would not be in the slightest bit relieved.
> Knowing that a *replica* of myself will be enjoying himself
> somewhere is not to know that *I* shall be doing so. For the
> continued existence of a person, more is required than
> replication.

(Davies 2004, 300)

Hick might reply that Davies is simply adopting at the outset the
view that replication is not identity, whereas in many cases we
are prepared to accept replication as a kind of identity. One can
have multiple performances of the same poem or symphony or
photograph, each of which may be said to be an authentic,
identifiable example of the poem, symphony, or photograph.
Perhaps being a person might be like being a computer program
that can be downloaded into a body: if it were your program,
the resulting person would have all you memories, desires,

beliefs, and so on. But, arguably, persons seem to be individual beings rather than programs, or scores that might be played by different musicians. Christian materialists can also consider two additional models.

The recreation model

Some Christian materialists believe God can and will recreate persons after they perish. On this view, your death truly involves your ceasing to be and yet at the appointed time God brings you back into existence. Persons have a unique essence or individuality, so God recreates you rather than a replica.

This is sometimes thought to involve 'gap-inclusive' continuity, according to which you can endure over time despite the fact that (for a short time) you ceased to exist. Merricks appeals to what might be called the uniqueness of divine creation. Imagine that God did create you. In doing so, God created *you* instead of some exact replica. If God created you at some time, can't God recreate you at another? Merricks writes,

> To do this, God didn't need to make use of matter that had previously been mine, for none had. To do this, God didn't need to secure my continuity, for [sic] any kind of continuity at all, with something I had previously been continuous with, because I hadn't previously been. And if God could see to it that I – not just somebody or other – came into existence the first time around, what's to preclude God from doing it again, years after my cremation.

(Merricks 2001, 197)

The idea that each individual person has an *essence* has some credibility. It seems plausible that each person has an essential core identity. Each of us appears to have what philosophers have called a quidity (a *thisness*) that is inviolable. If so, perhaps

Merricks is correct and we need not worry that the person recreated would be a mere replica.

There is at least one other option that does not need to be vexed by reassembly or recreation divine acts.

The reconstitution model

Lynne Baker has adopted a constitutional model of personhood. According to Baker, human persons are constituted by their bodies without being identical with them. An analogy that is often used is that statues are constituted by pieces of marble, copper, or bronze but are not identical with the substances that constitute them. Baker writes, 'A person is not a separate thing from the constituting body, any more than a statue is a separate thing from the constituting block of marble' (Baker 2000, 91). Because constitution is not identity, Baker contends that one can maintain both that persons are physical currently (they are composed of an exclusively physical body) and that they may survive the perishing of this body. Her position may seem puzzling at first, but in a common sense context we can readily distinguish between constitution and identity. The marble making up Michelangelo's statue *David* can be seen as a distinct object, for one could destroy the statue but still have the marble. Imagine you reconstruct the marble as Mickey Mouse: Michelangelo's masterpiece would be replaced by a Walt Disney character. Arguably, you might also slowly, over time, replace all the marble making up *David* until all the original marble was gone and yet the statue remained. These types of alterations suggest to Baker that a person might survive the dissolution of their body.

> The constitution view can offer those who believe in immaterial souls … almost everything that they want – without the burden of making sense of how there can be immaterial souls in the natural world. For example, human persons can survive

change of body; truths about persons are not exhausted by truths about bodies; persons have causal powers that their bodies would not have if they did not constitute persons; there is a fact of the matter about which … future person is I … The constitution view allows that a person's resurrection body may be nonidentical with her earthly body. According to the constitution view, it is logically possible that a person have different bodies at different times; whether anyone ever changes bodies or not, the logical possibility is built into the constitution view.

(Baker 2005, 387)

Baker seems to offer the logical possibility of survival without abandoning a materialist stance that, before death, human persons are composed of their physical bodies.

If any of these alternatives turn out to be possible, and not known to be false, then observing a human person dying is not ipso facto to observe a person cease to exist for ever. Although these materialist views have the advantage of according well with contemporary philosophy of mind (which tends to be materialist), some non-materialist accounts of persons and consciousness still have a credible claim to be taken seriously. Let us consider a non-materialist perspective, and then explore the relevance of a belief in an afterlife for the problem of evil.

One of the problems facing materialism is that it seems (at least until now) not capable of overcoming the apparently unique, non-physical character of consciousness and subjective experience. No observations or theories of the brain seem to reveal that consciousness is the very same thing as brain activity. We seem to be fully conscious, experiencing beings and yet it is not at all clear that consciousness and experience are identical with bodily states. We may have an exhaustive awareness of a person's purely physical states and processes and yet (without their testimony or the reliance of the testimony of others to establish correlation) have no idea of the person's consciousness or experiences. Clearly, a person's consciousness and experience are causally bound up with bodily states. Injury to the brain causes a rupture or termination of consciousness, but *causal dependence* and the *correlation* of bodily states and consciousness are not necessarily cases when there is an *identity* between consciousness and bodily states.

Consider the testimony of two materialists. Neither accepts a version of what is called dualism (there is a non-physical soul), and they are each frustrated by materialism. Colin McGinn writes of the apparent disparity of consciousness and physical things and processes:

> The property of consciousness itself (or specific conscious states) is not an observable or perceptible property of the brain. You can stare into a living conscious brain, your own or someone else's, and see there a wise variety of instantiated properties – its shape, colour, texture, etc. – but you will not thereby see what the subject is experiencing, the conscious state itself.

> (McGinn 1990, 10–11)

Consider now Michael Lockwood's observations about materialism:

> Let me begin by nailing my colours to the mast. I count myself a materialist, in the sense that I take consciousness to be a species of brain activity. Having said that, however, it seems to me evident that no description of brain activity of the relevant kind, couched in the currently available languages of physics, physiology, or functional or computational roles, is remotely capable of capturing what is distinctive about consciousness. So glaring, indeed, are the shortcomings of all the reductive programmes currently on offer, that I cannot believe that anyone with a philosophical training, looking dispassionately at these programmes, would take any of them seriously for a moment, were it not for a deep-seated conviction that current

physical science has essentially got reality taped, and accordingly, *something* along the lines of what the reductionists are offering *must* be correct. To that extent, the very existence of consciousness seems to me to be a standing demonstration of the explanatory limitations of contemporary physical science.

(Lockwood, 2003, 446)

Thomas Nagel and other philosophers might be cited on the difficulty of accounting for consciousness in a materialist framework. Materialism, then, is not without its problems. And some of the reasons for resisting a more expansive account of persons seem to be indecisive.

It used to be thought that if one believed that persons or minds or souls or consciousness were non-physical, then one could not account for the causal interaction of the mental and the physical. This objection seemed to have force so long as one assumed we have a stable model of physical causation, but increasingly it appears that contemporary physics allows for action at a distance and the positing of basic physical causal powers. If there can be basic (i.e. not further-explainable) causal powers on the physical level, why not in the non-physical realm? Moreover, there is no reason to think that dualism violates any known principle in physics such as the conservation of energy. Although a materialist, David Rosenthal contends that materialism is not justified because dualism violates a conservation principle.

Although the character of physics underlies one major argument, a specific principle of physics is sometimes thought to show that dualism is wrong. That principle states that in a closed physical system (that is, closed to other physical systems) the total energy remains constant. But if mental events are non-physical, then, when mental events cause bodily events, physical motion occurs uncaused by anything physical. And this, it seems, would result in an increase in the total energy in the relevant closed physical system. Mental causation of bodily events would conflict with the principle of the conservation of energy.

No such problem arises, even if dualism is true, when bodily events cause mental events. When bodily events cause mental events, presumably they cause other physical events as well, which enables energy to be conserved …

But [also] the dualist need not adopt the unintuitive idea that mental events never cause bodily events. Conservation of energy dictates only that the energy in a closed physical system is constant, not also how that energy is distributed within the system. Since mental events could effect bodily changes by altering that distribution of energy, the conservation principle does not preclude minds' having bodily effects.

(Rosenthal 1998)

The entry 'Materialism' in the prestigious *The Oxford Companion to Philosophy* captures the new, less-settled conviction that materialism is the simple philosophy of choice today:

Photons and neutrons have little or no mass, and neither do fields, while particles pop out of the void, destroy each other, and pop back in again. All this, however, has had remarkably little overt effect on the various philosophical views that can be dubbed 'materialism', though one might think it shows at least that materialism is not the simple no-nonsense, tough-minded alternative it might once have seemed to be.

(Honderich 1995, 530)

The current move to question the hegemony of materialism has led today to a partial revival of dualism. While I defined dualism above as the view that there is a non-physical soul, much more needs to be said.

'Dualism' is most sympathetically defined as the thesis that there is more to persons than the physical. If consciousness or the person is more than a physical body, then some form of dualism is right. (The way some define 'dualism', the term implies that the mind alone is valuable and the body is a mere appendage. None of this need be associated with the view that there is more to persons than bodies.) Those who go so far as to claim that the person is a substantial reality that can survive the destruction of the body are generally called *substance dualists*. Though it may be natural to claim that these dualists hold that a person is a non-physical soul, it is vital to appreciate that these dualists can affirm that in a healthy, embodied life the person is a functional unity; in other words, provided my body truly expresses my agency and is a suitable organ of sensory-perceptive awareness of myself and the world, to see my body is to see me. The soul need not be viewed as some spooky thing lurking behind or above the body. Only when the body and mind break down does there come about a division. If I were to lose all motor control and feeling except, say, to shake my head, my visibility or self-expression would shrink to only a partial embodiment.

Substance dualism provides a framework for a belief in an afterlife and has been largely the philosophy of choice for theists historically. It is also a view adopted by some non-theistic philosophers who believe in reincarnation. Let us consider one reason for embracing substance dualism which directly pertains to the afterlife. This is often called the *model argument*. There are four premises.

The first is a statement of what philosophers call the *indiscernability of identicals*.

1. If A is B, whatever is true of A is true of B.

This premise seems sensible. Take any number of identity statements: Mark Twain is Samuel Clemens, the Evening Star is the Morning Star, and water is H_2O. If there is a genuine identity between the two, whatever is true of one is true of the other.

To see Mark Twain is to see Samuel Clemens, the Morning Star is the planet Venus and so is the Evening Star, and to drink water is to drink H_2O.

The second premise applies the first premise to the person–body relationship.

2. If a person is his body, whatever is true of the person is true of his body.

This seems to be right, in my view. If I turn out to be my body (or my *living body*) then if my body weighs so many pounds, then that is what I weigh.

The third premise involves an affirmation of a possible state of affairs.

3. It is possible that a person can exist without their body and it is possible that their body can exist without the person.

This premise does not advance the claim that persons ever actually survive their bodies or their bodies survive the annihilation of persons. Imagine that there is in fact no afterlife. Even so, is it conceivable that an afterlife might exist – or, to put it differently, is it possible there could have been an afterlife? It appears we may imagine a person dying, the body perishing, and then the person surviving either in a disembodied state or in another body. (In this case we are imaging the afterlife on dualist terms, so to gain a new body would involve a person switching bodies rather than a person being replaced by a physical replica.) Novels like Charles Williams's *Ash Wednesday* contain narratives of such survival and people have actually reported having out-of-the-body experiences (OBEs). Let's again imagine that all OBEs can be accounted for chemically and none of the novelistic portraits of an afterlife is true. Nonetheless the descriptions of experiencing an OBE or afterlife seem to be coherent (they appear to represent bona fide possibilities). If we have no positive reason for thinking these states of affairs are impossible and we seem to be able to conceive of or picture or describe them, isn't it reasonable to believe they are possible?

Because of the importance and controversial nature of the third premise, let us not move ahead too quickly. Substantial intuitive support for premise 3 can be generated by the way we tend to view death. At the time of death, we usually do not think of the deceased's body as the person themself, but as a corpse or 'remains'. If, however, the person is identical with the body itself, then it seems that the person is still there after death (unless the body is annihilated). One may seek to avoid this by claiming that being a person equates to a fully functioning human animal body, and once the functioning has ceased then the animal body has ceased being a person. But this outlook seems puzzling, given the way we think of ourselves as subjects or selves. It appears (in ordinary experience) that you and I are individual beings and not modes of some other reality like an animal body. This will be called into question when we look at Buddhism in the next chapter, but at this stage I suggest that as long as we see ourselves as concrete individual beings who endure over time, then we do not appear to be a function or activity of something else. An analogy may be useful. We may speak of events like *dances* as though they are things or individuals (e.g. 'I enjoyed the dance last night'), but a *dance* is not so much a thing as a way people move. If being a person is a way the body moves, thinks, feels … then being a person is not being an individual. Arguably, that seems quite counter-intuitive. Our sense of ourselves as individual subjects is further vindicated by the fact that we understand ourselves as the same person over long periods of time despite the fact that our bodies change radically with the loss and replacement of cells.

If the above premises are reasonable, we can move to:

4. There is something true of a person but not true of their body.

And the conclusion is:

5. A person is not identical with their body.

A version of this argument was developed by René Descartes (1596–1650) and it has defenders as well as opponents today.

Let us consider four objections and replies.

The argument begs the question: Don't you have to already be a substance dualist to accept the third premise? After all, if you really believed the person *is* their body, why would you accept premise 3?

Reply: If you already know the person *is* their body, premises 3 and 4 will not be plausible, though many materialists concede that premise 3 seems coherent and seek to explain the apparent contingency of the person–body relationship. Of special interest are those materialists who actually accept premises 1–4 and yet resist substance dualism. As noted earlier, Lynne Baker, for example, believes that persons are composed of their bodies, and persons are not (now) non-physical but they can become non-physical. Is her view plausible? There is some reason to doubt that her constitution view is able to secure persons switching from a physical to non-physical constitution. After all, it seems implausible for some objects to persist through radical transformations. Would we say that the statue *David* persists if substituted by some kind of non-physical stuff (mental images or a hallucination)? This seems doubtful. Similarly it has been objected that it is implausible to believe a physical person could survive with a substituted non-physical 'body' (Zimmerman 2003, 340). Be that as it may, Baker's case indicates why the argument does not necessarily beg the question because she accepts the premises but tries (unsuccessfully, in my view) to avoid the conclusion.

A further reply is that if one is not already committed to 'person = body' identity, the thought experiment of imagining premise 3 can have as philosophically respectable a role as most philosophical analyses. In a typical argument in ethics, for example, a philosopher may advance the thesis that the property of goodness is the very same thing as the property of being pleasurable. A typical counter-example is then produced when it appears that we can imagine a state of affairs in which there is pleasure and no goodness or there is goodness and no pleasure. Such lines of reasoning help bring to light our awareness of values. Similarly, the person–body separability thought experiment can elucidate our grasp of ourselves and bodies.

Objection: The argument is only about concepts! Rather than establish person–body distinctness, the argument can only show that our concept of a person differs from our concept of our body. This seems very modest indeed. My concept of the Morning Star may differ from my concept of the Evening Star and yet it turns out both concepts refer to the same thing.

Reply: This objection would, if successful, undermine much ordinary, fully respectable reasoning. I can conceive of myself existing without the Eiffel Tower. Surely this is a reason to believe in the distinctness of myself and that global icon of France, and not merely a reason to think my concept of myself and the Eiffel Tower are distinct.

Objection to the first premise: In some cases it fails. For example, George W. Bush is the forty-third president of the United States, but not everything that is true of Bush is true of the forty-third president. For example, the forty-third president might have been Al Gore but this is not true of Bush.

Reply: This apparent counter-example only works if the term 'forty-third president of the United States' is treated as a general title for whoever happens to hold it. If the term is not used as a general title but specifically to pick out the person who actually is the forty-third president, then whatever is true of Bush is true of the forty-third president. (Note, too, that reference to you as a person or to your body is not a reference using a general title.)

Objection: Let us consider a religious reason to resist substance dualism, since this will naturally lead into a section on the value or significance of an afterlife. Christian materialists have argued that substance dualism is unable to account for the evil and horror of death. Trenton Merricks thinks materialists can more effectively see death as an enemy than as a release of a soul (1999, 284–5).

Peter van Inwagen has a similar objection: materialism entails that death is dreadful. 'When I think of the fact that I shall one day be composed of dead flesh, it is then that I appreciate the full power of the words of the medieval song: *Timor mortis conturbat me* ("The fear of death torments me")' (van Inwagen 1998, 63–4).

Reply: One can certainly be a substance dualist and a non-Christian (Peter Unger is a good contemporary example of a dualist who is an atheist) and so these objections need not detain all dualists. One might also be a substance dualist and hold that the person perishes along with the body. Addressing the objection more directly, one can be a substance dualist and hold that physical embodiment is a basic good. Arguably, having a life of integrated mental and physical processes is both itself good and the grounds for other great goods (e.g. making love, procreating, embracing …). One may also turn the objection around: dualism offers a philosophy in which death is not essentially a matter of a person coming to be 'composed of dead flesh'. Death in Christian philosophical theology is indeed bad, but it has also been seen as a transition to further life that, though it could be bad, may be quite good indeed.

I conclude this section with the claim that there are some plausible accounts of the afterlife given materialism, and if a non-materialist view of persons is coherent and credible, it, too, can offer an account of a person's survival of death.

What is the point of an afterlife?

Some atheists and theists believe that any conceivable afterlife is religiously and morally empty. Grace Jantzen writes,

> One might argue that only if it (the afterlife) is, is God just: the sufferings of this present can only be justified by the compensation of eternal life. But this, in the first place, is shocking theodicy: it is like saying that I may beat my dog at will provided that I later give him a dish of his favorite liver chowder. What happens after death – no matter how welcome – does not make present evil good.

> (Jantzen 1984, 40)

To some extent, Jantzen seems right, especially about the afterlife functioning in terms of compensation or justification. But what about the concept of redemption, alluded to in the last chapter?

Imagine a case of radical wrongdoing like murder. If there is no afterlife, the dead are extinguished for ever. There is no room for confession, restitution, forgiveness, and mercy. It is because an afterlife may permit such goods that many see an afterlife as an essential condition for the fulfillment of the purposes of an all-good God. In 'Jewish Faith and the Holocaust', Dan Cohn-Sherbok writes,

> Yet without this belief [in an afterlife], it is simply impossible to make sense of the world as the creation of an all-good and all-powerful God. Without the eventual vindication of the righteous in Paradise, there is no way to sustain the belief in a providential God who watches over His chosen people. The essence of the Jewish understanding of God is that He loves His chosen people. If death means extinction, there is no way to make sense of the claim that He loves and cherishes all those who died in the concentration camps – suffering and death

would ultimately triumph over each of those who perished. But if there is eternal life in a World to Come, then there is hope that the righteous will share in a divine life.

(Cohn-Sherbok 1990, 292–3)

One of the reasons why Jantzen does not see great value in an afterlife seems to stem from a narrow conception of what such a life might involve. She writes,

A paradise of sensuous delights would become boring: it would in the long run be pointless and utterly unfulfilling. We can perhaps imagine ways of making a very long feast meaningful; we do, after all, cope with lengthy terrestrial social occasions by choosing interesting conversational partners, and making the dinner occasions not merely for food and drink but also for stimulating discussion and for giving and receiving friendship the value of which extends beyond the termination of the dinner. But if the feasting literally never came to an end, if there were no progress possible from the sensuous enjoyment of paradise to anything more meaningful, then we might well wish, like Elina Macropolis, to terminate the whole business and destroy the elixir of youth.

(Jantzen 1984, 34–5)

Jantzen also resists the moral significance of an afterlife on the grounds that it may lead to reducing our central goal, which should be to seek fulfillment for ourselves and others in this life.

If we could go on pursuing an endless series of projects, it might not matter very much which ones we chose first: we could always do others later. Nor would it matter how vigorously we pursued them – for there would always be more time – nor how challenging they were or how well they developed us and brought out the best in us – for there would always be other opportunities. But if fulfillment is something which must be reached in this life if it is to be reached at all, we will be far less cavalier about the choices we make affecting our own fulfillment, and also, very importantly, in our relationships with others for whose fulfillment we are partly responsible.

(Jantzen 1984, 36)

Several replies may be promising.

First, most religious adherents to belief in an afterlife hold that if we neglect or harm the fulfillment (or well-being) of others and ourselves in this life, the consequences in a next life may be hellish. They also hold that even if all will be saved in the end, and opportunities for atonement extend into the next life, any idea that this would make one more relaxed in terms of good and evil would be a profound perversion. Perhaps the point can be made clearer in light of the belief that heaven and hell begin *in this life*. The afterlife is a continuation and transformation of the present. In this framework, for someone to be cavalier about pursuing good would be the equivalent of someone who is cavalier about creating their own hell.

Second, while it may be that feasting and other good activities may lose their goodness if they extend beyond a certain temporal period, are *all goods* so exhausted? What about the good of being a person? The good of a person's body may give out, but if a person is able to endure and delight in the goodness of endless variety (*bonum variationis*), it is not clear there would be any natural end point. I return to this point below.

Third, most religious metaphors for an afterlife (like feasting) are metaphors pointing to a good that goes beyond what we may conceive of now. Christians, for example, refer to the beatific vision – an experiential awareness of God – as an overwhelming, great good. Marilyn Adams proposes that an intimate relationship with God (which may begin in this life and extend into the next) may be a good that is incommensurate (incomparable) with any created good.

> The worst evils demand to be defeated by the best goods. Horrendous evils can be overcome only by the goodness of God. Relative to human nature, participation in horrendous evils and loving intimacy with God are alike disproportionate: for the former threatens to engulf the good in an individual human life with evil, while the latter guarantees the reverse engulfment of evil by good. Relative to one another, there is also disproportion, because the good that God *is*, and intimate relationship with Him, is incommensurate with created goods and evils alike. Because intimacy with God so outscales relations (good or bad) with any creatures, integration into the human person's relationship with God confers significant meaning and positive value even on horrendous suffering. This result coheres with basic Christian intuition: that the powers of darkness are stronger than humans, but they are no match for God.
>
> (Adams 1990, 220)

This understanding of goods goes far beyond Jantzen's survey of possible heavenly goods.

Apropos the problem of evil, the afterlife seems to provide a way of salvation beyond this world. But before we address such a possibility, let us consider the concept of the miraculous. Some concepts of the afterlife appear to involve special divine agency. Can it ever be plausible to believe in miracles?

Miracles?

An appeal to the miraculous has had a role in theistic treatments of the afterlife as well as in arguments for the existence of God (the appeal to miracles has been used to provide evidence of revelation or incarnation). Let us consider first the concept of a miracle and then some of the challenges of assessing reports of the miraculous.

In the eighteenth century, David Hume defined a miracle as a violation of the laws of nature brought about by a supernatural agent. This has been used by some theists, but it has also been criticized as failing to capture the religious significance of the miraculous. Not just *any* event that is caused by a supernatural agent would be considered a miracle. For this reason, contemporary defenders of an argument from miracles usually work toward a concept of the miraculous which does blend into more general considerations of religious experience but also does not become a merely mechanical, quasi-scientific notion.

To this end, a miracle may be defined here as an event brought about by God for a holy or divine purpose, an event that differs from God's general creative activity of sustaining the world and its laws regulating organic decomposition and regeneration. On this view, such normal regeneration would not count as a miracle, but God's causing an extraordinary event that differs from this regularity would do so. Grace Jantzen describes how this concept would work:

> If a situation arose in which there were compelling evidence for believing that Jesus rose from the dead, a revision of our supposed natural laws would hardly be the appropriate response … Where there is a single exception to a perfectly well established and well understood law, and one that is inexplicable unless one appeals to divine intervention (in which case it assumes enormous significance), what can be gained by making the nomological read, 'All men are mortal except those who have an unknown quality, observed on only one occasion and hitherto accountable for only by divine intervention.' … The skeptical response would be inadequate.

(Jantzen 1979, 325)

The theistic argument from miracles thereby works with concepts of agency and evidence, raising the question of when reported observations give us reason to believe that a good purposive agent is responsible for some event.

The best-known critic of the argument from miracles is David Hume. Hume's chief objection rests on a concept of intellectual responsibility:

> A wise man, therefore, proportions his belief to the evidence. In such conclusions as are founded on an infallible experience, he expects the event with the last degree of assurance, and regards his past experience as a full *proof* of the future existence of that event. In other cases, he proceeds with more caution: He weighs the opposite experiments: He considers which side is supported by the greater number of experiments: to that side he inclines, with doubt and hesitation; and when at last he has fixed his judgment, the evidence exceeds not what we properly call *probability*. All probability, then, supposes an opposition of experiments and observations, where one side is found to overbalance the other, and to produce a degree of evidence, proportioned to the superiority. A hundred instances or experiments on one side, and fifty on another, afford a doubtful expectation of any event; though a hundred uniform experiments, with only one that is contradictory, reasonably begets a pretty strong degree of assurance. In all cases, we must balance the opposite experiments, where they are opposite, and deduct the *smaller number* from the greater, in order to know the exact force of the superior evidence.

(Hume 1902, X, 1)

And Hume therefore concludes that 'the proof against a miracle ... is as entire as any arguments from experience can possibly be imagined'. The almost countless times we have observed human death as a natural, irreversible state (without resurrection) count as reason to believe that there has never been a death followed by a resurrection. His objection has been further defended by Antony Flew, J.L. Mackie, and others.

The most widespread theistic response to this objection has been to question whether Hume has simply begged the question. If one assumes at the outset that there have never been exceptions to the laws of nature, then one has assumed from the beginning that there have never been any miracles. It is not clear, however, whether Hume does beg the question in this fashion. Arguably, the strength of Hume's position is that he highlights the great weight of testimony on behalf of the laws of nature and the comparatively more slender testimony on behalf of exceptions to these laws. J.L. Mackie articulates this Humean strategy as follows:

> It is ... not enough for the defender of a miracle to cast doubt (as well he might) on the certainty of our knowledge of the law of nature that seems to have been violated. For he must himself say that this *is* a law of nature: otherwise the reported event will not be miraculous. That is, he must in effect *concede* to Hume that the antecedent improbability of this event is as high as it could be, hence that, apart from the testimony, we have the strongest possible grounds for believing that the alleged event did not occur. This event must, by the miracle advocate's own admission, be contrary to the genuine, more merely a supposed law of nature, and therefore maximally improbable. It is this maximal improbability that the weight of the testimony would have to overcome.

> (Mackie 1983, 25)

If Mackie is right, an argument for theism based on the appeal to miracles will always be at a disadvantage.

A second theistic reply is to challenge the use of probability employed by Mackie and other Humeans. Stephen Evans points out how Humean arguments presuppose a substantial background of philosophical commitments:

The defender of miracles may claim that whether miracles occur depends largely on whether God exists, what kind of God he is, and what purposes he has. Given enough knowledge of God and his purposes in relation to human history, occurrence of a miracle might be in some situations highly probable, or at least not nearly so improbable as Hume suggests ... In absence of any firm knowledge about God and his purposes, it would still be rash to claim with Hume that the probability of a miracle is vanishingly small. Rather it would appear more reasonable to conclude that it is hard, if not impossible, to estimate the a priori probability of a miracle; and therefore one should try to look at the evidence for miracles with a somewhat open, though cautiously skeptical, mind.

(Evans 1985, 113)

Evans and other theists such as Alvin Plantinga thereby place the debate about the miraculous in the context of an overriding debate between theism and naturalism.

Does this latter strategy completely undermine any evidential role for an argument from miracles? Not necessarily, for the argument can be seen as part of a broader, cumulative case for theism. The data advanced on behalf of theism might well be broadened to include not just religious experience, the contingency of the cosmos, and so on, but also certain accounts of what appears to be specific divine activity. The final outcome may resemble the argument for theism based on religious experience discussed in chapter 3.

An appeal to miracles has sometimes been challenged on the grounds that miracle narratives seem to support competing religious traditions. This raises the general question about how the different world religions should be considered in relationship to one another and to truth. This is also relevant to the problem of evil. Is there more than one valid religious path to enlightenment or salvation? Or do different religions set up exclusive alternatives?

One path or many?

John Hick is the leading opponent of treating religious traditions as exclusive competing paths to salvation. Hick contends that if traditional Christianity is true, then the majority of humanity is not saved. Hick asks, rhetorically, 'Is it credible that the loving God and Father of all … has decreed that only those born within one particular thread of human history shall be saved?' (Hick 1977, 179–80).

In place of what he sees as the narrowness of traditional Christianity, Hick believes that each religion can constitute a distinct but equally valued arena for achieving the shared religious goal of moving from ego-centered to reality-centered life. 'We can, I think, very naturally and properly see [the different world religions] as different forms of the more fundamental conception of a radical change from a profoundly unsatisfactory state to one that is limitlessly better because rightly related to the Real' (Hick 2000, 55–6). In Hick's view, different religions offer distinctive perspectives on the Real, each of which can free us from the bondage of self-centeredness.

On Hick's behalf, it may be argued that his reality-centered philosophy would seem to undermine religious conflict and create a religious foundation for tolerance. Evidence from miracles or religious experience would not favor one path as opposed to others, for more than one path may be valid.

Although Hick's position is deeply appealing, it may be that he overstates the problem with seeing religions as offering different accounts of reality, not all of which can be true. Keith Ward argues that different religions may offer different, complementary virtues and especially promote the virtue of humility as we appreciate our fallibility and the need to be open to others. He further argues that Christianity can recognize that the sphere of salvation extends farther than an encounter with Christ in this life. Christians can recognize that a loving God would seek the salvation of all even beyond this life (Ward 2000, 123, 125).

To employ the metaphor introduced in chapter 1 where religions are described as distinct worlds, perhaps God is active in the worlds of Judaism, Christianity, Islam, Hinduism, Buddhism, and other religious and secular contexts. Each world may contain authentic, deep values, and yet, if one of the theistic religions is true, the deepest fulfillment will be found (if only after death) in relation to God, whereas if theism is false and if Buddhism is true, enlightenment will not involve such a relationship.

An arena for the triumph of good over evil?

At least two lines of reasoning came into play in thinking about good and evil and the afterlife. One may be referred to as the *argument from love* and the second the *problem of restitution*.

The argument from love

There may be different forms of love (familial, romantic, friendship, and so on), but uniting most of them seems to the fact that when we love X (whatever it may be) we seem to approve or take pleasure in X. In the case of persons, this may be most clear: if I love you, I must in some way approve and take pleasure in your welfare. Conversely, I must disapprove of, or sorrow in, your harm. Of course, we can imagine circumstances that may complicate this thesis. Perhaps your undergoing a harm is in some way good for you and so disapproval and sorrow are not called for. But, setting aside such factors, consider this question: if we have reason to believe God loves persons, do we have reason to believe persons will have an afterlife? I suggest there is some reason to answer this positively. Earlier I suggested (*contra* Jantzen) that, though the good or value of a physical body may be exhausted, it is less clear that the good or value of a person may be exhausted. Imagine a person you love is dying but you have the power to heal them and to provide for them an arena in which to enjoy love and an abundance of goods. Unless we import to this thought experiment some peculiar additional factors (e.g. healing the person will cause others to die), then I believe love would lead one to effect the transformation. If love would lead us to take such action, wouldn't divine love (combined with omnipotent power) do that and more?

The problem of restitution

Another religious and moral rationale behind the value of an afterlife arises in the course of reconciliation. When one person harms another, there seems to be a series of steps that, ideally, contribute to reconciliation. The wrongdoer should confess the wrong and offer credible evidence of remorse along with a repudiation of any benefits received as a result of the wrong (e.g. return the money stolen). Presumably, too, the wrongdoer needs to develop new beliefs, desires, and intentions so as to provide evidence that they genuinely repent and seriously resolve not to do such an act again. Many other factors may have to come into play (perhaps punishment) and, ideally, the one wronged will need to accept the confession, among other things, but the crucial step that would need to take place in an ideal case is a restoration or full healing of the one harmed. Unfortunately, in human affairs this is nearly impossible, even in the case of trivial matters: I give a boring lecture and waste the time of my students. I can never restore to them that time. They will never be that young again. In more grave matters, the case is more evident. Imagine someone murdered your partner or sibling or child. The murderer may confess, repent, and so on, but they will not be able to do that which might centrally reverse the harm done: bring back the partner, sibling, or child to a full life of flourishing.

Judaism, Christianity, and Islam have addressed this universal human predicament with the teaching that what humans cannot do God can. So each religion has fostered a model of human reconciliation with other creatures and God which involves repentance and an active plea that God will mercifully heal creation. For Jews and Muslims who adopt this theology, salvation comes through God's restorative and omnipotent power, whereas Christians believe that this divine restorative omnipotent power is mediated and bestowed through the incarnation, Jesus Christ. Such restoration is not believed to *justify* the past wrong or to *eliminate the fact* that evil has occurred in creation. Divine restoration is rather best seen as a form of transforming (a combination of salvaging and healing) a damaged creation into a state of atonement (literally 'at-one-ment') with the nature of God. Judaism and Islam have historically rejected the idea that this restoration involved an incarnation, whereas Christians see the incarnation as the highest event and vehicle of divine redemption. But is it possible or even desirable that God become incarnate as a human being?

Incarnations and avatars

In the last section we considered Hick's moral objection to what might be called Christian exclusivism. If salvation is only possible through an overt encounter with Christ in this life, it seems that vast numbers of people are unfairly excluded from salvation. This difficulty may arise with many religions. If, say, enlightenment may only be found through Buddhism, then it may be an accident of birth whether you find enlightenment. It is plausible to think that if you are born into cultures where Buddhism is not taught, it is highly unlikely (but not impossible) that you will gain enlightenment. We have seen that some Christians address this problem by claiming that God works through many different contexts, calling people to salvation ultimately in relation to God though this may happen beyond this life. But even if this line of reasoning is persuasive, what about the claim that God became uniquely incarnate as Jesus Christ? Isn't there a kind of exclusivism in making *that* claim? Besides, some philosophers argue that it is impossible for God to become incarnate as a human being.

Some religious traditions counter the charge of exclusivism by claiming that there are multiple manifestations of God in diverse places. In Hinduism, for example, it is widely believed that Vishnu has descended to us in human forms called *avatāra* (Sanskrit for 'descent'). Vishnu appears as Krishna and Rama and in other forms to reveal divine glory and teach us the paths of wisdom. Some Hindus have even proposed that Jesus Christ was (is) an avatar of Vishnu. More on Hinduism in the next chapter.

So, one reply to the charge of exclusivism is to provide an inclusive understanding of divine manifestations. But for traditional Christianity, this route seems impeded by claims about the uniqueness of Christ as well as his full humanity. Krishna and other avatars do not seem to incarnate fully and irrevocably from birth to sacrificial death, being subject to all the human conditions of hunger, temptation, physical vulnerability, and so on. Christians can, however, claim that in affirming an incarnation in which God becomes fully human they thereby affirm the goodness (sacredness or hallowedness) of human life in all its particularity. Moreover, it is open to Christians to affirm (as most traditional Christian do) the *universality* of Christ's work. Most Christians believe that Christ's life, teaching, death, and resurrection are of universal significance and make restoration (salvation) possible for all persons. But is it even *possible* for God to become incarnate, given traditional theism?

One reason for thinking an incarnation is impossible rests in the apparent incompatibility of human and divine attributes. It appears that in traditional theism God exists necessarily and is thus without origin or birth, end or death. God is omniscient, omnipotent, omnipresent, and essentially good, whereas a human being is contingent. We are born and die. We are often ignorant, limited in power, limited to our bodies and immediate surroundings, and not only are we subject to temptation but most of us have caved in and done at least some wrongful harm to ourselves or others. To believe that a single person could have *both* sets of attributes, divine and human, seems like believing there could be a square circle.

There is not space to offer a full overview of the many ways in which Christians have responded to this charge. In brief, the traditional reply is to claim that although Christ is fully or wholly God (*totus dei*) Christ is not the entirety of God (*totum dei*). The belief that the Godhead is constituted by three persons (Father, Son, and Holy Spirit) and that the *incarnation* (from the Latin for 'taking on flesh') consists of the Son being born of Mary, as a human with all the limits in power, knowledge, temporality, appetites, desires, emotions, memory, and so on that comprises humanity. The claim is that in this incarnation Jesus Christ was fully human but not *only* or *merely* human. One way philosophers have sought to further articulate how a single person could have both human and divine attributes may be called the *mind within a mind model*.

In everyday experience, it seems we are able to adopt different roles or even personalities depending upon the occasion. You may be in a profession in which you cannot allow personal relationships to impact your behavior or emotions. As a professional, you simply have to set aside such personal desires and commitments and throw yourself wholeheartedly into your professional role. In this situation, we may say that your *mind* as a professional is a mind within your overall self or mind. That is, while remaining the same person over time (with *all* your complete beliefs and desires) you adopt a mind or identity that is far more focused and limited. The traditional belief in the incarnation involves more than believing God took on a role or profession or career. But it could be the case (some Christian philosophers argue) that while the Son retains omniscience, omnipotence, omnipresence, essential goodness, and necessary existence, as a member of the Godhead, the Son becomes incarnate as the mind–body reality of Jesus Christ with limited knowledge, power, and so on. The key element in this picture is that the incarnation has to be seen as no mere role-playing but as authentic and costly. On this front, traditional Christianity has opposed movements in the first century and later (like Gnosticism or docetism) in which the incarnation was seen as akin to an avatar or as incomplete. For example, some early Gnostics affirmed Christ as God in human form but they denied that he suffered or died. Orthodox Christians have affirmed, instead, the full humanity of Jesus in holding that he suffered, underwent temptation, and died.

The mind within a mind model has some plausibility. Other, related models might also be entertained in which it seems that a single person may contain or include a distinguishable identity or personality. Although not especially flattering, one may consider cases of supposed multiple personalities in which a single person can support a personality or identity distinguishable from the subject themself. Some philosophers also use the idea that a conscious person may have an unconscious that can function as an independent personality. These may partially assist the case for the possibility of believing that the second person of the Trinity retained all divine attributes while also coming to live a highly constrained human life. There remains, however, a vexing problem.

Let's grant for the sake of argument that God could come to live a human life of limited power, suffer, die, and so on. But if

Jesus is God, could Jesus truly have entered the human world of temptation? Part of the redeeming work of the incarnation is supposed to be Jesus's undergoing temptation and triumphing over evil. But if Jesus is divine and God is essentially good, it seems that God can do no evil. If Jesus is God and can do no evil, it seems that Jesus could not have been tempted. The problem may be formalized:

1. God is essentially good.
2. God cannot do evil.
3. Jesus is God (and human).
4. Jesus was tempted.
5. If a person is tempted to do evil, they must be able to do evil.
6. Either God is not essentially good, or Jesus was not tempted or not God.

If premises 1–5 hold then there is a contradiction. Not all the premises can be true.

Several replies have been developed. Some Christian philosophers deny the first premise. Others hold that in the incarnation the second member of the Trinity actually ceased being good essentially, thus allowing that it was truly possible for Jesus to have sinned or been wicked. Still others have questioned premise 5. The premise seems false if the evil in question involves an action. You may be tempted to commit adultery but cannot do so; imagine that you want to have an affair but you are on an inescapable island with only your spouse. But if evil includes desire, one may argue that simply desiring to break a marital vow is itself wrong or at least it seems less than perfect. Premise 5 might still be questioned, however.

Imagine you genuinely long for and find deeply attractive Pat, who is in a committed relationship with Chris (to use non-gender specific names). We might well consider this a genuine temptation to indulge in lust for Pat (a desire to possess her or him erotically) notwithstanding the fact that (let us imagine) you are constitutionally not a person who would or could let this longing or attraction lead to lust. In this case I am suggesting that the longing and attraction are not, ipso facto, wrong though lust would be.

Another example, however, may suggest that a straightforward desire to do what is wrong may be compatible with possessing a character that makes doing the wrong impossible. Imagine a different case. Mother Teresa is raising money for the poor and is staying at the house of a rich person surrounded by excess wealth he is not willing to donate for the poor. Imagine Mother Teresa has exhausted all her persuasive powers. Just before leaving she has an opportunity simply to take some of the man's money; she is certain it will not be missed; and she is positive that the money will do great good for the poor. Imagine, though, her taking the money would be wrong (involving, say, theft and deception). Wouldn't we expect Mother Theresa to be genuinely tempted to take the money, even if she is the sort of person who could not actually do so?

Should these examples be implausible, a Christian might simply take the line that in the incarnation Jesus' goodness was contingent and not essential or necessary.

Let us now look more closely at two non-Abrahamic religious traditions that originated in Asia.

6
Hinduism and Buddhism

Hindu and Buddhist philosophy of religion are becoming increasingly important in philosophy of religion as a whole. This is partly due to an increased appreciation of religious pluralism, the felt need to develop a 'global perspective', and also the intrinsically interesting philosophy that is being generated in Hindu and Buddhist tradition.

Hindu monism

According to monism (literally 'one-ism'), there is only one substantial reality as opposed to two (such as creator and creation) or a plurality of irreducibly different things. The most prominent form of monism in religion is the Advaita Vedanta school of Hinduism, of which the main exponent is Shankara (788–820).

In Shankara's view, Brahman is the supreme unsurpassable reality; the empirical, sensory world in which we seem to find ourselves is not the fundamental and final reality. Rather, this world may be described as a world of appearances. Brahman is in the world of appearances in that these appearances are the result of Brahman, but Brahman also simultaneously transcends this whole empirical domain and exists beyond any distinction, division, or change. The changes we observe and the distinctions we seem to draw with ease around the boundaries of objects (e.g. here is a person, there is a mountain) are the outcomes of our limited point of view. 'The world can be produced out of Brahman just as snakes are produced out of ropes and bent sticks are produced by water (by refraction)' (Koller [on Shankara] 1985, 90). A properly trained person who is not ignorant of the ultimate nature of things may see part of, or through, the illusion of plurality to the ultimate unity holding all things together. Hinduism thereby places great emphasis on cognition. Just as we are able to put away fear when we see that an apparent deadly snake is actually no more than rope, a realization that the world of appearances is not Brahman enables us to put aside worldly fears and seek our true identity elsewhere.

In monist religion, is this ultimate unity of all things – this comprehensive whole – conscious and/or personal? For Shankara and most advocates of Advaita Vedanta, ultimate reality transcends consciousness and personality altogether. As noted in chapter 1, Hindu tradition includes important strands in which ultimate reality is described in theistic terms and there is an acknowledged distinction between Brahman (conceived of as the creator of the cosmos) and the cosmos itself. Ramanuja (1017–1137) sought to affirm the reality of that which was below Brahman, and Radhakrishnan (1888–1975) sought to harmonize these two strands of Hinduism, monist and theist, holding out for both the unity and distinguishability of objects. His views are certainly monist in the end, however: 'There is nothing else than the Absolute which is the presupposition of all else' (Radhakrishnan 1960, 119):

> So far as the Absolute is concerned, the creation of the world makes no difference to it. [The world] cannot add anything to or take anything from the Absolute. All the sources of its being are found within itself. The world of change does not disturb the perfection of the Absolute.
>
> (Radhakrishnan 1936, 502)

Whereas in theism the principal mode of understanding the cosmos is in terms of creation, monist systems – such as those advanced by Radhakrishnan – describe the visible world as more of a manifestation or emanation, or, if you will, a divine evolution, rather than a creation. 'Creation' comes from the Latin *creare* for 'to produce, bring forth, beget'; 'emanation' is from the Latin *e* for 'from' and *mano* for 'flow'; and 'evolution' is from the Latin for 'to roll out', *volvere*.

At least at the outset, monism appears to be radically false. In common experience, it seems that individual persons are indeed different (I am not you) and diverse spatiotemporal objects are diverse. In the West, it is often held to be axiomatic that everything is itself and not something else. As Bertrand Russell once commented, 'The universe is all spots and jumps, without unity, without continuity' (Russell, cited by Ewing 1985, 207). Must all versions of monism be seen as completely undermined by this perspective?

Some monists are prepared to think their views are truly in opposition to common sense and no worse off because of it. In Advaita Vedanta Hinduism, the justification for monism is built principally on religious experience and the authority of the Vedic scriptures. This provides a way of liberation for the soul, which comes to understand itself as not wedded to the illusions of this world, but at one with that which is truly ultimate. This is not a repudiation of using 'common sense' in 'common circumstances', but a rejection of thinking of such common sense as revelatory of the deepest levels of reality (there are deeper accounts of why things are as they are, and deeper, greater values). Do such monist accounts or others need to be seen as radically at odds with common sense? Let's consider one strategy to accommodate common sense within monism.

In recent philosophy there is considerable debate as to how to weigh competing conceptual schemes, each of which may be used to describe what exists. This is sometimes called 'the division problem'. How should reality be divided? Why do we group some object within one category as opposed to another?

> Our language divides up reality in a certain way, though we can apparently describe an indefinite number of other ways this might be done. This fact may not in itself be seen as generating a philosophical problem, for it may merely suggest the need for an empirical explanation, in terms of psychology or sociology, of why our division practices are as they are. A philosophical problem is generated, however, by certain normative intuitions which we seem to have about these practices. Intuitively, it seems that there are good reasons why we ought to have essentially the division practices we do have; it seems that it would be in some sense incorrect or irrational for us to employ a language that divides reality in some way significantly different from our ordinary way. The philosophical problem is to explain what these normative intuitions amount to, and to determine whether they can be properly defended. What, if anything, makes our division practices more correct or rational than various alternative practices we seem able to describe? This is what I am calling the division problem.
>
> (Hirsch 1993, 3)

Much argument in the philosophy of science, language, and mind is focused on this division problem. Clearly, the division problem calls for a sophisticated response. Some of our classifications seem straightforward reflections of human desires (e.g. consult any dictionary definitions of 'garbage' or 'weed' or 'pollution'); others do not (e.g. geometric shapes). Let us focus on the prospects for unification rather than entirely on the problem of division.

Consider the following move by a monist. Let it be granted that the best of the natural scientific schemes of the world should be adopted, not as true in their formulation of 'ultimate reality', but instead as pragmatic, empirical ways of ordering our experiences, making predictions, and controlling outcomes. The monists need not deny that separable, distinct persons 'exist', in the sense that contexts arise in which referring to them as distinct, non-identical objects is fully justified. What monists may seek to do, then, is reinterpret these pragmatic claims as intelligible in light of a deeper, transcendent unity; it is a matter of substance versus mode of being. This concept could use some further unpacking.

One way to spell out this position is by a grammatical illustration. Imagine a shift in grammar. In English we distinguish between subjects, adverbs, and adjectives. Adjectives modify subjects and do not stand for objects in their own right. There is no such object 'big' but there can be a 'big tree'. We routinely refer to a host of things that are granted honorary subject status that can be reinterpreted as adjectives. Thus we may speak of the swiftness of a dance or the pain in a leg or the minty taste of tea, but these may all be understood as *ways people move*, *the way one's leg feels*, and *the way mint tea tastes*. We may so keenly reify references to dances as 'things' that it seems odd to insist that what we are referring to are not 'things' but modes of being or acting or sensing. It seems quite natural to think of there being an odor in a basement, for example, as though it is one thing among others: the odor is over there! But this way of talking does not give one serious pause when it comes to reinterpreting or re-analyzing one's claims in terms of what the basement smells like to someone who goes down there.

Let us entertain the following experiment (an exercise that is very different from the argument of the last chapter that selves are substantial individuals): think of individual objects (the mountain, river, you, and me) not as subjects pure and simple, but as ways in which the universe is at various stages. The universe is mountaining, to put it very awkwardly. On this analysis, the things we take to be subsistent objects (subsistence comes from Latin *subsistere* for 'to continue') become something similar to waves, configurations of something deeper, something more unified, something that binds us together. Waves exist continuously or endure over time, but their individuality is a matter of the shape and movement of a body of water. Individual objects are thus continuously shifting incarnations (modes or manners) of something else. Back to the charge that 'everything is itself and not something else': does monism fly in the face of this dictum? Not necessarily – the monist can argue that the modes of God or Brahman are distinct and not identical, notwithstanding the fact that each mode is a reflection of a singular reality. Consider one more example of the difference between a mode and a substance. What is more fundamental: a hand or a fist? The reason we think the former is more basic is because 'a fist' refers to how a hand may be shaped. But imagine we treat a fist as a thing. It would be distinct from an open hand, which would be distinct from hundreds of other ways we may shape our hands. Here you would have only one reality (a hand) that may yet be treated as underlying hundreds of different 'things'.

As Vinit Hasksar observes, a Hindu monist can distinguish between ordinary life and life as observed and experienced at the deeper levels of mystical awareness:

> But it is wrong to claim that in fact the average Hindu sees himself in his ordinary life as one with Brahman. The view that he is one with Brahman is one that he may aspire to comprehend; with the exception of the sages and the mystics it is a truth that people are, at best, only dimly aware of. His ordinary life is so full of his egoistical drive, which is why he needs to be reminded by himself and by others of deep truths which stress his identity with the cosmos. According to the doctrine of *Advaita* there is indeed just one Brahman or the cosmic self pervading us all, but as long as the people are in the grip of

Maya or illusion they will believe that they have separate egos
and attach themselves to illusory goals.

(Hasksar 1991, 89)

At the mystical stage of perception, however, monists in Hindu
as well as Buddhist tradition highlight the absorption of the
individual into Brahman or Nirvana. Consider this passage from
the Hindu *Brihadaranyka Upanishad*:

[A]s a lump of salt cast in water would dissolve right into the
water ... so, lo. Verily, this great Being [*bbuta*], infinite, limitless, is just a mass of knowledge. Arising out of these elements
[*bbuta*], into them also one vanishes away ... For where there is
a duality, as it were, there one sees another ... Where, verily,
everything has become just one's own self ... then whereby and
whom would one see?

(2, 4, 12, 14)

Consider, too, Suzuki's description of the ultimate absorption
into that which is ineffable:

The individual shell in which my personality is so solidly
encased exploded at the moment of satori. Not necessarily that
I get unified with a being greater than myself or absorbed in it,
but that my individuality, which I found rigidly held together
and definitely kept separate from other individual existences ...
melts away into something indescribably, something which is of
quite a different order from what I am accustomed to.

(Suzuki 1933, 18)

But it may be argued that this vision need not be reflected in a
denigration of non-absorbed, individual life.

As observed earlier, Hinduism is diverse, and so sometimes
one finds Hindu philosophers like Ramanuja affirming the

indissolubility of the person – what he refers to as 'the consciousness of the "I"'.

> To maintain that the consciousness of the 'I' does not persist in the state of final release is again altogether inappropriate. It, in fact, amounts to the doctrine – only expressed in somewhat different words – that final release is the annihilation of the self. The 'I' is not a mere attribute of the self so that even after its destruction the essential nature of the self might persist – as it persists on the cessation of ignorance; but it constitutes the very nature of the self. – Moreover, a man who, suffering pain, mental or of other kind – whether such pain be real or due to error only – puts himself in relation to pain – 'I am suffering pain' – naturally begins to reflect how he may once for all free himself from all these manifold afflictions and enjoy a state of untroubled ease; the desire of final release thus having arisen in him he at once sets to work to accomplish it. If, on the other hand, he were to realize that the effect of such activity would be the loss of personal existence, he surely would turn away as soon as somebody began to tell him about 'release' ... Nor must you maintain against this that even in the state of release there persists pure consciousness ... No sensible person exerts himself under the influence of the idea that after he himself has perished there will remain some entity termed 'pure light'! – What constitutes the 'inward' self thus is the 'I,' the knowing subject.
>
> (Thibaut, I, i, 1, in Radhakrishnan and Moore 1967, 547)

Ramanuja thereby insists that the very quest for release is the release *of* the 'I', not *from* the 'I'. But in order to promote the possibility of transcending one's individual 'I', consider the following argument. (I do not endorse this argument, but I find it intriguing and helpful to foster the appeal of monism.)

In what may be called the *rotation argument* consider the following question: Could you have been another person? Is it possible for *you* to have been Napoleon, for example? Try to imagine you were born in 1769 to some minor Corsican nobility. Picture what it might have been like to be a junior officer and then slowly to rise through the ranks. Speaking for myself, I think I can imagine what I gather the world looked like to Napoleon and though I do not relish identifying with someone responsible for one million French soldiers dying under his leadership, not to mention millions of other soldiers and civilians killed, it seems to me I could have been Napoleon. Isn't imagining you could have been another person an element that arises in reading novels, watching films, or hearing stories? In reading compelling autobiographies, don't we often imagine the life of another person from the inside, as though that life was our own? C.S. Lewis once observed that part of the point of literature is to see through other people's eyes and hear through others' ears, and so on (1992). I believe that given the right information, aesthetics, and empathy we can imagine being a different gender, having different parents, and more.

I will state the first premise of the rotation argument using myself:

1. I could have been Napoleon.
The second premise is:

2. Charles Taliaferro could not have been Napoleon.
Charles Taliaferro was born in New York City in 1952, not in Corsica; he has been to Waterloo Station in London, but not the battlefield; etc. What follows? 'I' refers to something other – perhaps something deeper – than 'Charles Taliaferro'. Perhaps the latter refers to what we might call a *lifetime*, whereas the 'I' refers to some deeper identity, for we can use our imagination to expand well beyond Napoleon. If I could have been Napoleon, couldn't I have been any number of different people? Provided we seem to be able to imagine such states of affairs, and

given the principle outlined in chapter 3 about when it is reasonable to believe a state of affairs is possible, we seem to have reason to believe that 'I' refers to more than Charles Taliaferro. And the same holds for you when you use the first-person pronoun and you imagine the possibility of being someone else.

Objection: This thought experiment makes as much sense as asking me to imagine I was a mountain range or train; substitution of persons has no intuitive plausibility as a genuine possibility. This can be brought to light if we ask: Would you, as Napoleon, invade Russia? It appears that you are compelled to say you would; otherwise, you would not have been Napoleon, because that in fact is what Napoleon did. But once you see that the state of affairs you express in the premise 'I could have been Napoleon' amounts to simply 'I could have all his properties', then the premise seems to collapse into something like 'If I was a mountain, I would be a large land mass', which is absurd. You could not have been a mountain, and it is just as certain you could not have been Napoleon, for you are Charles Taliaferro or Jane Doe or whichever non-Napoleon figure you are.

Reply: Correct – a thought experiment of imagining becoming a mountain or a train makes no sense. But isn't this because in most cultures mountains and trains are non-persons and have no consciousness or subjective experience? Being a mountain does not feel a certain way. And yet when we come to persons and personality, doesn't our imagination reach further? As for the question of whether you or I, as Napoleon, would have invaded Russia, I am inclined to see some sense to the question. A historian might well seek to place themself in the position of Napoleon and consider the following: if I had his resources, beliefs, desires, advice, personality, and opportunity, would I have invaded? This kind of speculation might even be indispensable in building up a full historical portrait of Napoleon, flushing out his desire for self-glory and the glory of an empire.

There is another response to this argument which could have been developed by Ramanuja himself. When I imagine myself being Napoleon, Ramanuja might well agree that I am imagining a bona fide possibility and yet claim that what I am imagining is my *self* or *soul* having a different body, different birth and parentage, and a different history. I am not thereby imagining myself actively switching selves or souls or 'I's, but switching bodies and histories. So Ramanuja would claim that if *I* could have had the role Napoleon played, then the one who is Charles Taliaferro could have played the role the Napoleon played.

Though the rotation argument may not succeed as an argument, perhaps it still succeeds in drawing attention to how monism seems to lead us to a greater, deeper identity than our particular selves. Let us consider some of the implications of this broader outlook.

Love, Duty, and Glory

Unifying a great deal of Hindu ethics is the importance of disciplined, mindful activity. Whether or not one embraces the full release of the self or retains the self in illumination, persons are bidden to not give themselves over to reckless passion. The *Katha Upaniṣad* declares,

> Know that the Self is the owner of a chariot, and the body is the chariot itself; know that the reason is the charioteer and that mind, indeed, is the reins …
>
> The man whose charioteer is discernment and who reins in his mind,
>
> he reaches the end of [his] journey …
>
> (*Katha Upaniṣad* 3.3.9, in Monius 2005, 333)

The moral teachings that lie behind such pronouncements are not, however, what appears to be a dry moralism, but are a loving apprehension of the divine. In 'Differentiations in Hindu Ethics', Maria Heim summarizes this by citing a medieval bhakti poet:

Knowing one's lowliness
in every work;
the spray of insects in the air
in every gesture of the hand;
things living, things moving
come sprung from the earth
under every footfall;
and when holding a plant
or joining it to another
or in the letting it go
to be all mercy
to be light
as a dusting brush
of peacock feathers:
such moving, such awareness
is love that makes us one
with the Lord
Dasarēśwara

> (translated from the Kannada by Ramanujan 1973, 54–5, cited in Heim 2005, 353)

One way to appreciate the implications of a Hindu perspective for one's self is by focusing on the concept of glory. In the West, glory (in Greek, *kleos*) has a rich history going back to Homeric poetry. In the *Iliad*, glory has a troubling role as the name for praiseworthy acts on the battlefield with the bloody defeat of one's enemy. Glory was even linked to the shield or sword you might take (perhaps bloodied) from your fallen opponent. In the *Iliad* and *Odyssey* you may read a subtle critique of glory and a celebration of hospitality (*xenia*) and homecoming, but glory still appears to be the seductive object of a warrior's desire for immortality through poetic remembrance and praise. In the beloved Hindu text the *Bhagavad-Gita* there is also an engagement with glory and war.

The *Bhagavad-Gita* (from the Sanskrit for 'Song of the Lord'), composed around the sixth century BCE, is principally made up of a dialogue between a warrior, Prince Arjuna, and his charioteer Krishna. A war is about to begin between two armies. As the dialogue begins, Arjuna confesses his despair about war, his fear of killing, and confusion. Krishna counsels Arjuna on the call of dharma, living in harmony with one's duty. Arjuna is not immediately persuaded, though he receives ongoing instruction, learning that through devotion, action, meditation, and knowledge he may come to be released from his ego-driven passions. Krishna further teaches him that physical death is not the absolute end of the person, for one must endure many births on the path of enlightenment. Arjuna's full deliverance from dejection occurs when Krishna displays the glory of his universal form.

> You are the primal God, the most ancient Person. You are the ultimate resort of all the universe. You are the knower, the object of knowledge, and the supreme abode. The entire universe is pervaded by You, O Lord of the infinite form. You are the controller of death, the fire, the wind, the water god, the moon god, and Brahmaa, the creator, as well as the father of Brahmaa. Salutations to You a thousand times, and again and again salutations to You. My salutations to You from front and from behind. O Lord, my obeisances to You from all sides. You are infinite valor and the boundless might. You pervade everything, and therefore You are everywhere and in everything.

> (*Bhagavad-Gita* 11:36–45, trans. Ramanada Prasad)

Upon seeing the glory of the divine, Arjuna is enabled to return to his duty. Glory had purged Arjuna from self-blame, confusion, and ego-centered fears.

There are definite, plausible pantheistic and panentheistic interpretations of the *Bhagavad-Gita* (e.g. in chapter 9, Krishna says, 'all beings are in me') as the soul is led to give up one's 'false self' and identify with the immortal soul or Atman.

One thing to be appreciated here is how individual self-concern and fear are challenged by two things: the immense glory of the divine and the charge that a person's true selfhood lies in relation to the divine.

The vision of the glory of Krishna in the *Bhagavad-Gita* displaces the Homeric kind of glory that selfishly seeks praise and renown through conflict. It also eclipses a person's desire for self-glory through reputation, quieting what medieval Western philosophers referred to as the inordinate desire for pre-eminence and that today we might call *celebrity*. The glory of 'the primal God' clearly chastens individual pride, but the *Bhagavad-Gita* does not annihilate self-will. Note how the role of duty and worth is not destroyed by Krishna's revelation. Arjuna is not left in a state of absolute debasement before divine glory. The final outcome, however, is a realization that doing one's duty is a role one must play that is important, but it is not itself the divine glory. One may have a humble pride in carrying out one's duty. Divine glory thereby regulates or governs a fitting, ordinate commitment to one's dharma.

Regrettably, the concept of glory (human and divine) has not received the attention it deserves in the current literature in philosophy of religion, political thought, and elsewhere. Unquestionably, 'glory' has had an important cultural role (East and West), whether this is in connection with the divine or imperial temporal power, and I commend 'glory' as a topic for further inquiry.

As for the idea of a false or true self, I suggest that one can well make sense of such a distinction. One's false self can be said to be one's ill-thought-out character that is largely based on false beliefs and useless passion. If I pride myself in possessing some excellence I lack, there is a sense in which I am attaching myself to an illusion, rather than being anchored in what is authentically fulfilling. I might also be detached from my true self insofar as I have utter self-loathing and dejection as a result of a false, diminished view of my value. The idea that freedom from bondage involves coming to one's true self suggests that the final end – saving state – is akin to coming home. One has to come to where one belongs.

Buddhism also raises concern when persons act in light of illusions and become wrongly attached to ego. Let us first consider a Buddhist view of the self and then take note of one aspect of Buddhist ethics.

No-Self in Buddhism

In chapter 4 we took up what many think is the most difficult obstacle facing theism: the problem of evil. (Buddhist philosophers have traditionally argued against some Hindu views of Brahman based on the problem of evil.) For Buddhism, the persistent philosophical challenge rests in the concept of the self. It appears that Buddhism denies the existence of the ego or substantial self. Consider this early text:

> Whether Buddhas arise, O priests, or whether Buddhas do not arise, it remains a fact and the fixed and necessary constitution of being that all its constituents are transitory. This fact a Buddha discovers and masters, and when he has discovered and mastered it, he announces, teaches, publishes, proclaims, discloses, minutely explains, and makes it clear, that all the constituents of being are transitory ... Whether Buddhas arise, O priests, or whether Buddhas do not arise, it remains a fact and the fixed and necessary constitution of being, that all its elements are lacking in an ego [substantial, permanent

self-nature]. This fact a Buddha discovers and masters, and when he has discovered and mastered it, he announces, teaches, publishes, proclaims, discloses, minutely explains, and makes it clear, that all the elements of being are lacking in an ego.

> (*Anguttara-nikiaya*, iii, 134, in Radhakrishnan and Moore
> 1967, 280; the text is Theravadin)

A similar stance appears in the *Visuddhi-magga*:

> Just as the word 'chariot' is but a mode of expression for axle, wheels, chariot-body, pole, and other constituent members, placed in certain relation to each other, but when we come to examine the members one by one, we discover that in the absolute sense there is not chariot; and just as the word 'house' is but a mode of expression for wood and other constituents of a house, surrounding space in a certain relation, but in the absolute sense there is no house; and just as the word 'fist' is but a mode of expression for the fingers, the thumb, etc. in a certain relation; and the word 'lute' for the body of the lute, strings, etc.; 'army' for elephants, horses, etc.; 'city' for fortifications, houses, gates, etc.; 'tree' for trunk, branches, foliage, etc.; in a certain relation, but when we come to examine the parts one by one, we discover that in the absolute sense there is no tree; in exactly the same way word 'living entity' and 'ego' are but a mode of expression for the presence of the five attachment groups, but when we come to examine the elements of being one by one, we discover that in the absolute sense there is no living entity there to form a basis for such figments as 'I am' or 'I'; in other words, that in the absolute sense there is only name and form. The insight of him who perceives this is called knowledge of truth.

> (*Visuddhi-magga* xviii, in Radhakrishnan and Moore 1967,
> 284–5; the text is Theravadin)

The difficulty arises in squaring this view of the self with reincarnation.

In much of the traditional teaching about reincarnation or the transmigration of souls in Hinduism and Buddhism, there is a central concern with karmic justice according to which goodness is rewarded and evil punished. Those who act ethically receive a reward, whereas the wicked receive punishment. Consider a representative, Buddhist text:

> Now, people here whose behavior is pleasant can expect to enter a pleasant womb, like that of a woman of Brahmin, the Ksatriya, or the Vaiśya class. But people of foul behavior can expect to enter a foul womb, like that of a dog, a pig, or an outcaste woman.
>
> (*Chandogya Upanṣiad* 5.10.7, in Heim 2005, 345)

M. Hiriyanna describes the implication of the Law of Karma as it is borne out in practice:

> The law of karma accordingly is not a blind mechanical law, but is essentially ethical. It is this conviction that there are in reality no iniquities in life which explains the absence of any feeling of bitterness – so apt to follow in the wake of pain and sorrow – which is noticeable even among common people in India when any misfortune befalls them. They blame neither God nor their neighbour, but only themselves for it. In fact, this frame of mind, which belief in the karma doctrine produces, is one of the most wholesome among its consequences. Deussen refers thus to the case of a blind person whom he met once during his Indian tour: 'Not knowing that he had been blind from birth, I sympathized with him and asked by what unfortunate accident the loss of sight had come upon him. Immediately and without showing any sign of bitterness, the answer was ready to his lips, "By some crime committed in a former birth."'
>
> (Hiriyanna 1951, 48–9)

The problem is that if the individual person does not exist over time, how can it make sense for the person to be the subject of karmic justice over many lives? Bruce Reichenbach concludes his close study of karma with this summation:

> To conclude, we have argued that there is an ambiguity in the Buddhist account of the human person. On the one hand, personal identity is merely ascribed; selfhood is a fiction. We are easily misled into thinking that there is personal identity and continuity when in fact there is nothing but series of events. This perspective entails that rebirth is a fiction, as are the doctrines of karma and liberation. On the other hand, the doctrine of karma is held to have empirical content; karma and liberation are experienced realities. This perspective entails that the person is reborn. We have seen that it falls to karma to provide the object ground for the personal identity and continuity found in rebirth. These two hands are not consistent. Is the self a fiction or not?

(Reichenbach 1990, 132)

The dilemma may be put this way: If the self is not a fiction, then reincarnation and karma may be coherently described, but then a fundamental teaching of Buddhist tradition and some Hindu tradition (Advaita) is in jeopardy. But if the self is a fiction, then the process of reincarnation is difficult to defend consistently.

There are several replies. One is to treat the Buddhist concept of *anatta*, or no-self, as not so much a philosophical teaching as a spiritual counsel. At one point when the Buddha is asked whether there is or is not a self he seemed to rescind either stance (*Samyutta Nikaya* xliv:10). What Buddha may be teaching here is that we should direct our attention to freeing ourselves from harmful, useless desires. The counsel, in other words, has more to do with our identification than with whether or not we are selves. Who you are may be seen as a reflection of what you identify as yourself. You may identify yourself as an athlete or dancer – and thus see yourself in fundamentally bodily terms – or you may see yourself as a theoretical mathematician for whom bodily life is a necessary but not very interesting condition. One way to read the concept of *anatta* is that we should set aside this preoccupation with the identified self. We should instead cultivate selfless (or egoless) compassion.

A second approach is to delimit levels of reality. The self in this temporal world of change, rebirth, and redeath is partly constituted by a unity of momentary states. This self exists but at what Malcolm David Eckel identifies as a level of convention. The self, at this level, has true moral significance and responsibilities even though, at a deeper, ultimate level, there is no self. In 'Responsibility without a Self', Eckel writes,

> Most Buddhists deny that there is any real continuity from one moment to the next. Objects, experiences, and personalities are nothing but momentary events, like the flickering moments in a candle flame. They may produce the illusion of continuity, but they are actually nothing but a series of momentary events. This view of things, reminiscent of Heraclitus, maintains that you cannot step into the same river twice. Some Buddhists push the argument further and contend that not only is there no 'stream'; there are no real moments. I think of this as the view that you cannot step into the same river once. No matter which side you take in this intramural Buddhist debate, there ultimately is nothing to bear responsibility from one moment to the next.
>
> The stress in this sentence falls on the word *ultimately*. There *ultimately* is no self, if by *self* we mean something that lasts long enough to experience regret or to be hauled into court and told to answer for its crimes. But there is a distinction in Buddhist philosophy between things that are true *ultimately* and things that are true *conventionally*.

(Eckel 2007, 30)

This distinction between the conventional and the ultimate may leave moral responsibility in a precarious place: is the duty to be just but a duty for a conventional self? Eckel argues that the denial of a substantial self actually assists the project of establishing moral responsibility. He uses a story about the Buddha and Angulimāla to make his point.

In the town of Kosala a child is born who is corrupted by a teacher to undertake the grotesque take of killing people in order to collect their fingers. The killer, whose name means 'garland of fingers' (Angulimāla), then encounters the Buddha. In this encounter, the killer repents his harmful ways and seeks to become a monk. After this conversion, Angulimāla begs for food in the villages he used to torment. The people are quite understandably upset and fearful.

> When Angulimāla turns to the Buddha for help, the Buddha tells him to perform an 'act of truth' – to say: 'As I have never harmed a living creature since I was born in this noble life, may your life be spared.' Angulimāla asks how he can possibly say this after all the violence he committed against the villagers. The Buddha says that Angulimāla stopped being that person he was when he became a monk. Angulimāla pronounces the words, and the woman is saved. To this day, apparently, Angulimāla's words are used as a charm in Sri Lanka to ease a woman's pain in childbirth.

> (Eckel 2007, 29)

According to Eckel, the Buddhist denial of the self, at the level of ultimate reality, allows for such a moral, spiritual transformation. I leave it to you (as with virtually *all* the arguments in this guide) to measure the benefits and promise of such a strategy. One might well argue that believing in a substantial self can allow for profound moral reform (or moral regeneration or renewal) while still maintaining sufficient personal identity between Angulimāla the killer and the reformed Angulimāla. Still, the opposition to a substantial self is not limited to Buddhism. One can find diverse philosophers arguing for a non-substantial view throughout the modern era in Western philosophy, from David Hume in the eighteenth century to Derek Parfit today.

To summarize this section: so long as we cling to the self as an enduring substantial reality, it does exist (at least conventionally at the level of common experience or as a desired object) through reincarnation, until finally released in a state of Nirvana. But because of karmic law the unified self cannot simply be released the way one would solve a puzzle. Most forms of Buddhism stress the vital role of compassion and merit in the quest for karmic justice and release from the clinging, desirous self. Let us consider one way such merit is understood.

The transfer of merit

In the history of Buddhism there gradually evolved the concept of how the compassionate merit of one person can provide a bounty or treasury that can be given to another who lacks merit. Malalasekera explains how the ideas of *parivatta* (transferring merit) and karma can coincide in Buddhism:

> The act of sharing one's good fortune is a deed of compassion and friendliness and, as such, very praiseworthy and meritorious … The recipient of the transfer becomes a participant of the original deed by associating himself with it. Thus the identification of himself with both the deed and the doer can sometimes result in the beneficiary getting even greater merit than the original doer, either because his elation is greater or because his appreciation of the value of deed is more intellectual, and therefore more meritorious … What is significant is

that in order to share in the good deed done by another, there must be approval of it and joy in the beneficiary's heart … Here, too, as in all actions, it is the thought which, according to Buddhism, really matters.

(Malalasekera 1967, 86, cited in Holt 1981, 16)

The idea that the merit of a person's acts can create a treasure to draw upon was first introduced in connection with providing karmic merit to ancestors. But it soon expanded, especially in relationship to Pure Land Buddhism, a movement within Mahayana Buddhism. Whereas earlier forms of Buddhism stressed monastic, rigorous discipline, Pure Land Buddhism was more capacious in its teaching that ordinary people may attain Nirvana through the worship of Buddha Amida ('Amida' is his Japanese name; in Sanskrit it is 'Amitabha'). This Buddha of Light and Life is believed to dwell in a land of bliss (Sukhavati) and provide the means of liberation by sharing his abundant wisdom. Anyone who calls on his name in faith (without any karmic works of his or her own) will be cared for by Amida's merit.

The idea that one may transfer merit may seem counter to the Buddhist notion of karmic works, for karma seems foundational to a Buddhist explanation of suffering through reincarnation and desert. Arguably, however, there is no compromise, given the idea that a person may – through compassionate action – create a surplus of merit, enabling others to receive this merit even if they have none themselves. In some Buddhist teaching, the transfer of merit requires that the recipient must call out the name of the Buddha, whereas in other teaching the Buddha may confer merit on those who make no such explicit petition.

Does the concept of the transfer of merit make sense in a Buddhist or non-Buddhist context? I suggest that it does in both. Consider a non-Buddhist, secular case in which you have been wronged by a person (Pat). Imagine Pat shows some remorse, but the injury to you was so grave that you continue to blame Pat and contemplate legal compensation. Then Chris enters the scene. Long ago, you wrongly injured Chris, but, rather than blaming you and seeking compensation, Chris displays such compassionate love for you that you naturally come to confess your wrong, undergo remorse, and resolve to do good works. Chris then asks you to forgive and care for Pat. Wouldn't the 'merit' of Chris's act transfer, giving you good reason to respond lovingly (or try to) in your relationship with Pat?

If such a transfer makes sense in a secular context, there seems to be coherence in terms of karma and the distribution of good works. Christians in the West may have difficulty with the concept of transferring merit because of the abuse of such a notion at the time of the Reformation when the Roman Catholic Church sought to sell indulgences – essentially, this was a guarantee of reducing the punishment of souls in the next life by appealing to the treasury of merit created by the saints. Protestants objected that there can be no surplus of merit, for God calls for our full devotion; one does not get 'extra credit' for saintly works. In reply, it should be appreciated that the transfer of merit in Buddhism is not subject to commerce; the transfer is free. It may also be important to stress that Christians themselves often accept a transfer of merit in at least one central case: Christ. The transfer of merit may not be a point of tension between Buddhism and Christianity; it may instead be a point of poignant similarity. The similarity is so strong that I suspect that a Christian's experience of the compassionate merit of Jesus might be appreciated as similarly illuminating and compelling as a Buddhist's experience of the compassionate merit of Buddha Amida. It seems a live possibility that both Buddhist and Christian may (or may not) authentically experience a transcendent compassion.

Philosophy of religion in the East

In the classical Western text *The Metaphysics*, Aristotle proclaims that we human beings have a natural desire to know. Even quite apart from the utility of such knowledge, we love sensory awareness for its own sake. One can discover a similar respect for the inherent value of knowledge in much of Indian philosophy, but there is also a distinctive emphasis on pursuing knowledge and philosophical inquiry for the sake of the good or liberation (*moksa, mukti*) from distress (*duhkha*) and the cycle of rebirth and redeath. In the course of articulating a theistic philosophy earlier (chapter 2) I sought to correct Dawkins's thesis that in the 'God Hypothesis' the concept of goodness is an 'add-on' and not central to theism. A similar point needs to be made about Hindu and Buddhist philosophy: their pursuit of the good is not an unintended addition to the process of philosophical inquiry.

In 'Darsana, Anvíksikí, Philosophy', Wilhelm Halbfass demonstrates that although traditional Indian philosophy has produced theoretical work on the magnitude of Aristotle, there is also a stress on how this work may lead us to fulfillment and to avoid suffering. Halbfass stresses the soteriological (saving) role of Hindu and Buddhist thought: 'Indian philosophers tend to emphasize that the cognitive motivation is inseparable from the desire to obtain what is pleasant and to avoid what is unpleasant; just as human activities in general, intellectual, cognitive endeavors are said to be directed towards "fruits" or "results" (*phala*)' (Halbfass 2003, 302). To employ Dawkins's vocabulary, in what might be called the 'Hindu or Buddhist Hypotheses', goodness is no mere 'add-on'.

Language and the sacred

In Hindu and Buddhist philosophy, there is some reflection on the limits of language. If Brahman is believed to transcend all differentiation – as it is in the Advaita Vedanta tradition – then it appears that no linguistic description of Brahman is possible. Meaningful language seems to require identity and difference. As Aristotle argued in the fourth century BCE, meaningful statements of any kind (e.g. 'justice is a virtue') only have meaning if their contradiction is false ('justice is not a virtue'). But if some concept of the sacred (Brahman or Nirvana) is held to be beyond such differentiation, how is meaningful discourse and reflection to proceed?

Asian philosophy of religion has taken several paths concerning language about the sacred. One is to retain identity and difference when it comes to the sacred and stress the difference between contradictions and contraries. A contradiction does not appear to allow for middle ground; if the word 'square' has a fixed reference, everything is either square or not-square. Apples as well as cities, numbers, and concepts are either square or not-square. Contraries are different: A and B are contraries if A is true, B is false, and vice versa, but it is possible neither are true. Let A equal 'It is night' and B equal 'It is day.' In ordinary English, if it is day, it is not night and vice versa, but it may be that neither is the case; it could be dusk. Using this distinction, a philosopher may defend a claim such as 'Brahman is neither good nor evil' as meaningful insofar as it asserts that Brahman is beyond the categories of good and evil. This claim is different, however, than the claim that Brahman is good and not-good. One approach would be akin to maintaining a balance of the apophatic and cataphatic, as sketched in chapter 2.

Another response is to see philosophy as a tool to expose some of the problems, perhaps even contradictions, in our ordinary assumptions about the world, thus leading us to be open to that which extends beyond the world of appearances. Some Buddhists use such a technique as a prelude to meditative practices that involve altered states of consciousness.

A related, further response would be to see a role for philosophy – as the love of wisdom – in cultivating reverential silence before the sacred. To that end it seems fitting to cite at the end of this chapter perhaps the most well-known Asian statement about the sacred transcending language. In the Tao Te Ching by Lao-tzu (551–479 BCE) we read,

> The tao that can be told
> Is not the eternal Tao.
> The name that can be named
> Is not the eternal Name.

7
Morality, politics, and religion

Might it be the case that objective morality requires the existence of a good God? In Dostoevsky's novel *The Brothers Karamazov*, one character claims that without God everything is permitted. Is this thesis cogent? After addressing this central question, let us consider the opposite charge that some secularists pose today: If God is believed to exist, could it be that almost *anything* might be justified? If one believes God has commanded you to X (shut down abortion clinics, oppose homosexual marriage, refuse blood transfusions, etc.), is X then your moral duty? It is because of the worry that religion can generate abundant justifications for harmful practices that many political liberals seek to limit the role of religion in public policy. The chapter then moves on to present what may be a promising framework in which to assess and compare religious and secular values: the ideal observer theory. This is relevant to questions about what should be the relationship between politics and religion. In a pluralistic liberal democracy, is it permissible for religious believers to advance public policy on religious grounds not shared by secular society at large? I conclude with three case studies of when secular ethics might benefit from an encounter with religious ethics.

A religious foundation for ethics?

Moral requirements like the duty not to kill or the duty to keep promises and so on can naturally be thought of as commands.

Following one's conscience can even feel as though one is following an 'inner voice' of some kind. Could it be that moral duties are themselves reflections of the will of a good God, so that the moral requirement 'Do not kill the innocent' is the equivalent of or stems from 'God prohibits the killing of the innocent'? Some philosophers have argued that the most reasonable account of the realm of morality is that it is constituted by divine commands and prohibitions. On this view, moral duties receive their binding character from the agency of the creator and, in the absence of God, morality would lose its objective authority. This stance has been developed in strong and moderate forms of a divine command theory of ethics and in the context of Platonic theism.

According to what might be called the *strong divine command theory*, there is an essential identity of morality and divine commands. What it means for someone to claim that killing the innocent is wrong is that God prohibits this. We have here a strict identity just as in the case of an analytic definition or in an identity relationship in the natural world. In terms of definitions, a 'grandmother' simply is 'a female whose child has a child', and in natural identities water simply is H_2O. Similarly, so it is argued, to claim something is wrong is to claim that God prohibits it. The divine commands may be formatted as follows:

X is morally wrong = God prohibits X
Y is morally right = God commands Y
Z is morally neutral (neither good nor bad morally) = God
    neither commands nor prohibits Z

Why think this strong thesis might be true? It would anchor ethics in that which is beyond human culture. A divine command theory allows us to say that something is wrong even if a human culture approves of it. This account also seems to ground ethics at the very heart of reality. The purpose of ethics is intended by the creator of the universe. H.P. Owen grants that although ethical precepts (keep promises, do not murder) seem like impersonal structures, they are best seen as personal commands.

> [Moral] claims transcend every human person and every personal embodiment. On the other hand we value the personal more highly than the impersonal; so it is contradictory to assert that impersonal claims are entitled to the allegiance of our wills. The only solution to the paradox is to suppose that the order of [moral] claims, while it appears as impersonal from a purely moral point of view, is in fact rooted in the personality of God.
>
> (Owen 1965, 53)

One difficulty is what might be called the *good atheist objection*. Aren't there atheists who grasp moral rightness and wrongness and act accordingly? This might not be decisive, however, because a person might be an expert on the use of water and yet ignorant of atomic theory. The deep structural foundation for ethics may not be evident to everyone who thinks ethically. And so the existence of ethical atheists is not, itself, a good objection to the strong divine command theory. But there is another problem: the Euthyphro Dilemma.

In the fourth century BCE Plato constructed a dialogue, the *Euthyphro*, which included a question that can be slightly rephrased: is X good because God loves it or is X loved by God because it is good? The problem with *X is good because of God's love* is that it then seems that love gives rise to reasons, and we may face this problem: what if God loved something unjust? If God loved cruelty, would cruelty then be right? Some have been prepared to go some of the way with this proposal and charge that if God did command cruelty then it would be morally right and yet (they argue) God did *not* command cruelty. This reasoning may suffice, but many philosophers worry about the coherence of someone (even God) making something morally right by decree. Commands can, under certain conditions, create new obligations as when someone who owns land offers a decree (imagine they prohibit hunting), but we rarely think these commands can create obligations that are contrary to objective rights and wrongs. We would be uneasy with a landlord who could simply make murder right.

There is another version of the divine command theory that may be more successful. According to a moderate form of the theory, for *X to be morally right* amounts to *X is commanded by an essentially good God*. On this view, goodness is not defined by God's commands. God is held to be good in God's self and the source of all goodness. In this framework murder is evil and compassion good, and necessarily so, but their necessary objective status is derived from God's commands. This version of the divine command theory avoids the problem of caprice; God cannot, by God's very nature, command murder. But it still insists that these normative, objective truths stem from God.

Why should one adopt such a framework? It offers a unified, stable account of values as stemming from a single source. It makes no use of an appeal to God's sheer power; in other words, the obligatory nature of divine commands does not stem from an appeal to God's power, e.g. obey God or face intolerable consequences.

A difficulty with this theory arises in making clear the kind of causal relationships involved between God and objective moral norms. Causal relations are often thought to be contingent, but this is not always the case. Some determinists hold that *all* causal relations are fixed and Spinoza claimed that the whole cosmos could not be other than it is.

There is yet a third alternative that may be called *Platonic theism* which resembles the moderate divine command theory but does not claim that the objectivity of morality rests on God's commands. On this view, God is essentially good, and yet moral rightness and wrongness do not depend on God's commands. Nonetheless the very existence of a cosmos in which there are objective moral duties and values rests upon God's causal creativity. The objectivity of morality, then, is not derived from God, but the existence of a universe of moral beings is itself purposively willed by God. Morality and values have a *teleological structure*: their very existence and the ultimate fruition of the pursuit of values are part of God's intentional will.

If the strong version or moderate version of the divine command theory holds, then ethics and values do depend upon God. Given that God necessarily exists, the question raised at the beginning of this chapter (if God does not exist, would everything be permissible?) would not arise because there is no possibility of God's non-existence. If Platonic theism turned out to be true, then ethics would have a cosmic intelligibility or purpose that naturalism would neither allow nor concede. Let us compare theistic and naturalistic ethics.

Ethics with or without God

There are a host of moral theories that seem neutral in terms of whether or not God exists. So, according to a popular form of *utilitarianism*, happiness (or pleasure or preference-satisfaction) is a great good, and morally right and wrong actions can be understood in relation to their promotion or impeding of such happiness. For a *deontologist*, moral duties are fundamental. According to perhaps the most famous deontologist of all time, Immanuel Kant (1724–1804), we each have a duty always to act in a way that treats each person as an end in themself; you might use someone (e.g. asking for directions) but should not thereby denigrate their dignity or treat them in a way that is incompatible with them being valuable in themselves. It seems as though either moral theory could be viable in a theistic or non-theistic framework. Still, some theists have held that in a naturalist framework objective values are not as easily aligned with nature.

George Mavrodes and C. Stephen Layman have both proposed that naturalism does not offer as 'deep' or coherent a treatment of values as theism. Mavrodes employs Bertrand Russell's famous portrait of a cosmos without God:

> That man is the product of causes which had no prevision of the end they were achieving; that his origin, his growth, his hopes and fears, his loves and his beliefs are but the outcome of accidental collocations of atoms; that no fire, no heroism, no intensity of thought and feeling, can preserve an individual life beyond the grave; that all the labors of the ages, all the devotions, all the inspirations, all the noonday brightness of human genius, are destined to extinction in the vast death of the solar system, and that the whole temple of man's achievement must inevitably be buried beneath the debris of a universe in ruins – all these things, if not quite beyond dispute, are yet so nearly certain that no philosophy which rejects them can hope to stand. Only within the scaffolding of these truths, only on the firm foundation of unyielding despair, can the soul's habitation henceforth be safely built.
>
> (Russell, cited by Mavrodes 1986, 215)

In a Russellian cosmos, the moral duty to be just and compassionate may indeed be stringent, but such duties would not in any way accord with what may be called *cosmic purpose*. From the standpoint of the cosmos, human and other forms of life count for zero. The paleontologist–theologian Pierre Teilhard de Chardin (1881–1955) drove home the implications of a Russellian naturalism with the concept of 'total death':

> Multiply to your heart's content the extent and duration of progress. Promise the earth a hundred million more years of continued growth. If, at the end of that period, it is evident that the whole of consciousness must revert to zero, *without its secret essence being garnered anywhere at all*, then, I insist, we shall lay down our arms – and mankind will be on strike. The prospect of a *total death* (and that is a word to which we should devote much thought if we are to gauge its destructive effect on our souls) will, I warn you, when it has become part of our consciousness, immediately dry up in us the springs from which our efforts are drawn.
>
> (de Chardin 1969, 43–4)

By way of contrast, most theistic religious traditions affirm that God works to redeem or save that which is good in this world and beyond.

As noted in chapter 5, a traditional theistic framework of an afterlife involves restoration, regeneration, and judgment. Contemporary theists take up different views of hell and heaven. Most defenses of hell in the literature are grounded on the belief that hell involves the voluntary election of some persons to embrace evil (Peterson 1992, 124–5). On the other hand, there are some *universalists* who hold that no one would, finally, choose hell. Thomas Talbott and Marilyn Adams have argued that though a person may temporarily choose evil (or hell) God will ultimately lead each person to embrace concord with God's love (heaven). But, whether one adopts universalism or a more strict view of retribution and freely willed alienation from God and the good, theists offer an overall view of reality in which an ethical life is grounded in and fulfilled by God's good, purposive will.

Naturalists can entertain a variety of replies. One is simply to hold the line and contend that morality, by its very nature, is binding whether or not it is backed up by a cosmic purpose. A naturalist might also counter that it is perhaps the brevity of natural life that intensifies its value: we should act well with each other now, for before long we may all perish. This line of reasoning seems especially promising. A naturalist may have to entertain the possibility of cosmic tragedy (in the end our moral projects, like all projects, will vanish), but that should make us all the more loyal and stringent about what does matter to us morally. Alternatively, a naturalist might hope that humanity and other life may endure for ever and there never will be a time of total death.

The debate over the objectivity and authority of ethics in naturalism has recently taken an interesting shape. Some naturalists have allowed for a very broad emergence of consciousness and values from non-conscious, valueless forces. This more than allows for a revived teleological argument: Does naturalism wind up positing so many levels of emergence (consciousness, moral values, aesthetic values like beauty) that the natural world is better accounted for by theism rather than naturalism? But if a naturalist elects to allow for only minimal emergence, can objective values be successfully grounded? Michael Ruse, for example, is a neo-Darwinian evolutionist who holds that 'morality is just an aid to survival and reproduction, and nothing more' (Ruse 1989, 268). This outlook may face a problem similar to the Euthyphro objection: if cruelty aided survival and reproduction, would cruelty be good?

Naturalists have offered a counter-argument to the thesis that ethics requires a religious foundation. They contend that religion can hamper or undermine moral reflection.

Can religion be bad for your ethics and politics?

Most readers, I imagine, will answer this with a confident 'yes'. People have been hated and persecuted for what appear to be religious reasons (e.g. burning heretics, witch trials, crusades, holy war), and I will not try to fully counter this with examples on the other side. I will, however, offer an account of why religion may be thought to have such a big impact ethically, and then I will challenge the way in which the charge of religious cruelty is framed.

In addition to the divine command theories, one reason why religious reasons are viewed as morally relevant involves the claim that God owns the cosmos, and, as such, God is within God's rights to direct the lives of creatures. I briefly present the thesis of divine ownership and offer a sprinkling of objections and replies.

Divine ownership of the cosmos is upheld in the Hebrew and Christian Bibles (1 Chronicles 29:11–18; Psalms 24:1, 50:12; Ezekiel 18:4) and the Qur'an ('To God is the personal ownership [*mulk*] of the heavens and the earth', from 'The Light'). The thesis that the cosmos is owned by God is a key claim in medieval philosophical theology and much modern theology. It has led both to an amplified sense of duties (i.e. do X not just because it is good in itself but also because you belong to God and God commands X) but also to new duties such as the duty not to commit suicide (with possible rare exceptions).

Among modern philosophers, probably the most well-known advocate of divine ownership is John Locke (1632–1704), who developed his stance in the *Second Treatise on Civil Government*. Locke held that 'we owe our body, soul, and life – whatever we are, whatever we have, and even whatever we can be – to Him [God] and Him alone ... God has created us out of nothing and, if He pleases, will reduce us again to nothing' (Locke, in Idziak 1980, 182). Locke's position has been defended by Richard Swinburne, Baruch Brody, and others. It is because of divine ownership that it would be conceptually impossible for God to steal from creation. None of us has a right to property over against God's rights. Thomas Aquinas held this: 'What is taken by God's command, who is the owner of the universe, is not against the owner's will, and this is the essence of theft' (Aquinas 1947, Ia2ae, 94.5). Swinburne draws the following conclusion: 'It follows from this that it is logically impossible for God to command a man to steal – for whatever God commands a man to take thereby becomes that man's and so his taking it is not stealing' (Swinburne 1993, 207).

Appeals to divine ownership have often been used by theists to undermine what is believed to be excessive individualism and to foster a greater sense of the duty to aid others. Historically, the theistic appeal to give to others in need has often been preceded by advancing the thesis that all one's possessions are conferred as a gift by God. This theme of the creation as a gift runs through Jewish, Christian, and Islamic traditions. Lenn Goodman singles it out in his summation of Jewish philosophy:

> Through all the change of style and structure, and all the seeming change of paradigms, the thematic content [of Jewish philosophy] remains remarkably steady, anchored in tradition and text: God offers love and demands justice and generosity. Life is a gift; truth, a sacred and inescapable responsibility.
>
> (Goodman 1995, 431)

Divine ownership ethics has its critics. A chief objection is that such an ethics seems to make human beings slaves to God and this offends a mature view of our autonomy and dignity (Young 1977; Lombardi 1984). One defense of divine ownership maintains that being owned by God is not pernicious. Another defense is to revise the divine ownership ethics so that it amounts to a weaker claim that persons belong to God.

As for the first defense, it may be argued that God is essentially good and thus not subject to capriciousness and injustice. Any analogy with human enslavement is therefore wide of the mark. Being owned by God would be like being owned by goodness. Consider the second possibility: In English the term 'belonging' can be used both to indicate property and also to make a value judgment. When someone reports that 'Chris belongs in this school' or 'Chris and Pat belong in this family' there is a suggestion that there is a fitting propriety to being in certain relationships. It is good or in some way deserved for Chris and Pat to be in school and in the family. The ownership of God thesis can be modified to make the claim that persons belong to God in the sense (a) that they exist, in part, because God conserves them in being (life is a gift) and (b) that a life of fulfillment and welfare is to be found in relationship with God (for further material on divine ownership see Brody 1974; Avila 1983).

From a secular point of view, belief in the ownership of God may give rise to some ethical difficulties. If God owns the cosmos, cannot God intend for some land to be the domain of some people rather than others? In part, it is because theism can generate expanded ethical duties that some political liberals are seriously committed to limiting the role of religion in policy-making. Arguments supporting this separation of state and religion have been advanced recently by Robert Audi, Richard Rorty, John Rawls, Ronald Dworkin, and others. Here the goal is to restrict the reasons that are acceptable in political decision-making only to those who are capable of being appreciated independent of recourse to comprehensive, religious conceptions of the cosmos. Jeremy Waldron states the aim of liberalism as follows: 'Liberals demand that the social order should in principle be capable of explaining itself at the tribunal of each person's understanding' (Waldron 1987, 149). In the same spirit, Audi countenances only secular reasons in public, political decision-making: 'A secular reason is, roughly, one whose normative force, that is, its status as a prima facie justificatory element, does not (evidentially) depend on the existence of God (for example, through appeals to divine command) or theological considerations (such as interpretations of a scared text), or on the pronouncements of a person or institution *qua* religious authority' (1989, 278). John Rawls adapts a similar position. In public life, when making political decisions that affect society at large,

> we are to appeal only to presently accepted general beliefs and forms of reasoning found in common sense, and the methods and conclusions of science when these are not controversial … We are not to appeal to comprehensive religious and philosophical doctrines – to what we as individuals or members of associations see as the whole truth – nor to elaborate economic theories of general equilibrium, say, if these are in dispute.
>
> (1993, 224–225)

Rawls and other liberal political theorists thereby seek to secure a sharp distinction between religious and political discourse.

There are several difficulties, however. First one may challenge the delimitation of 'comprehensive religious and philosophical doctrines' from 'common sense'. It may be argued that 'common sense' can itself count as a comprehensive doctrine (such as religious views of life). Moreover, it may be argued that if we are to banish from political decision-making all theories of the cosmos and values unless they are held by *every reasonable person*, then very little will be left standing. Is there any consensus in the United States, Great Britain, and other democracies about utilitarianism, deontology, natural law, the ideal observer theory, and so on? Arguably not. As R.M. Adams writes, 'nothing in the history of modern secular ethical theory gives reason to expect that general agreement on a single comprehensive ethical theory will ever be achieved – or that, if achieved, it would long endure in a climate of free inquiry' (1993, 97). If we allow any of the ethical theories just cited to count as worthy of use in political decision-making, why cannot the divine command theory or Buddhist ethics also have a role to play?

Against the secularism of Locke, Stephen Macedo points out that 'Locke does not really succeed ... in fashioning arguments capable of convincing those who regard a supportive social and political environment as crucial to salvation' (Macedo 1993, 623). A key difficulty that faces contemporary political liberalism is that many in society define themselves in religious terms. For those who do, the liberal ideal seems not only unmotivated but based on a suspect account of the individual. The identities of many individuals are shaped by the communities in which they live and are at radical odds with a religiously barren secularism.

In the next section I articulate a framework that may help bring together religious and secular value theory and address the liberal worry about religion fostering dangerous views about God's commands. But first let me briefly return to the charge that religions are responsible for so much cruelty in the world.

To what extent does one's claim to be a member of a religious tradition make one a member? In standard reference works you will find estimates of Christians (2.1 billion), Muslims (1.5 billion), Hindu (900 million) and so on, but if we look below these statistics, we must ask: when is one, say, a Christian or Muslim or Hindu? In chapter 1, I suggested that one's identity in a religion is open to serious challenge to the extent that one's action and character deviate from the canonical authoritative teaching of the religion. So, as John Locke argued in *The Letter on Toleration* (1689), someone who claims to be a Christian and yet hates other people is not actually a Christian. Locke uses as part of his argument the New Testament teaching that 'He who says he is in the light, and hates his brother, is in darkness – He who loves his brother abides in light – But he who hates his brother is in darkness and walks in darkness, and does not know where he is going because the darkness has blinded his eyes' (I John 2:9–11; Locke cited just verse 9 but I have quoted the fuller context). One may similarly argue that a Muslim who does not care for others is at least inconsistent and not a practicing Muslim, for Muhammad teaches, 'No man is a true believer unless he desires for his brother that which he desires for himself' (Ibn Madja, Intro. 9). Because the golden rule is prevalent in virtually every extant religious tradition, one may argue that any self-identified 'religious' advocate may not be authentically religious if they live in violation of the golden rule. For a representative collection of such golden rule teachings, consider:

> One should never do to another that which one would regard as injurious to oneself. This, in brief, is the rule of Righteousness.
>
> (Anushana parva 113:7)

> As a mother cares for her son, all her days, so towards all living things a man's mind should be all embracing.
>
> (Sutta Nipata 149)

> Do not do to others what you would not live by yourself.
>
> (*Analects* xxi, 2)

> One should 'regard [others'] gains as if they were his own, and their losses in the same way'.
>
> (Thai Shang 3)

> What is hateful to yourself do not do to your fellow man. That is the whole of the Torah.
>
> (Babylonian Talmud, Shabbath 31a)

This list of similar teachings may be extended indefinitely.

It may be objected that this suggested approach does away with the secular critique of religion too quickly. If the above strategy were adopted, then there can be no cases of selfish religious adherents who despise their neighbors. Perhaps the best approach is a middle way: flagrant violation of ethical religious teaching (e.g. the golden rule) undermines one's religious identity, but there may be cases when persons and communities diverge from such teaching and can be critiqued as religious entities. A plausible case might be the charge that Christianity is guilty of anti-Semitism. Although Jesus and the founders of Christianity were Jewish, one may (in principle) argue that many Christians have shown disrespect for Judaism from the first century onward. This appears to be a plausible and important point of reference in Jewish–Christian dialogue when representatives of Christianity have confessed and set out to repent of past anti-Semitism.

An ideal observer theory

In setting the stage for a comprehensive moral framework that may include religious and secular values, I highlight the three components that seem to constitute, in part, moral reflection, West and East, North and South. It will be useful to extrapolate from a modern setting. I will advocate the theory that follows, but also field a range of objections.

Imagine you and I are arguing over some action (X) in which I think X is morally permissible and you think X is morally impermissible. We will each probably bring into focus different facts. If our argument is over the use of nuclear power as a source of energy, I may argue that you resist it because you are employing a faulty physics, a mistaken probability calculus, and an exaggerated and unrealistic view of risk-taking, and so on. You may reverse the charges on each of these fronts and bring in facts I have neglected. Imagine, for example, I have failed to see that in modern nuclear energy policy more risk is placed on the economically disadvantaged than on the privileged. I may also be working with the implicit assumption that energy policy involving risks is voluntarily imposed in a democracy. You point out that this imposition will, in practice, always be imperfect and in some cases essentially flawed (for example, children and the severely impaired cannot function as independent parties voluntarily accepting risks).

Early on in a moral dispute much of the work will go into identifying different facts, either challenging what one or both of us presume to be factual or bringing to bear new, not commonly recognized facts. A disputation of facts is often tied in with an appeal to impartiality.

Even if you and I agree about what I am calling the facts involved in nuclear energy, disagreement may still occur owing to partiality. Imagine I come from a country that benefits strongly from nuclear energy. My country places other people at risk who do not benefit from this energy practice. You may tell me that I have failed to carry out an essential element in the thinking behind the golden rule of putting myself in another person's shoes. Would I *still* favor the use of nuclear power if, say, the roles were reversed and I were receiving the burden without the benefit?

An appeal to impartiality and facts does not cover all the elemental stages of moral reflection. There is also an affective dimension, an appeal to *what it is like* to be an agent or victim or bystander. In approving of nuclear energy policy, am I taking seriously (affectively incorporating) what it would feel like (or be like) to suffer from radiation sickness, to give birth to a child suffering from radiation poisoning caused by a China syndrome (a core meltdown), or to be that child? Presumably it is because of the perceived need to take the affective dimension seriously in moral reflection that those of us in wealthy countries sometimes fast in order to remind ourselves (albeit in a fragmented and highly artificial way) of the needs of those who live with chronic hunger. In the city where I live, there are programs you may enter in which you are placed in economically destitute settings for short periods in order for you to get some hint of what it might feel like to be homeless. In my schooling as a child we were sometimes asked to go through the day in a wheelchair or wear a blindfold in order to get some feeling for what it might feel like to be physically impaired. Such practices may seem like pathetic examples of merely simulating experiences that can be employed in moral reflection, but I can report that such educative practices have shaped my own and other students' perspectives.

In classical theism God is understood to be necessarily existing, omnipotent, eternal, the free, gracious creator and sustainer of the cosmos, worthy of worship and the object of our supplications. These features do not (as yet) enter the above portrait of moral reflection. But in theism God is also pictured as all-knowing, which is understood to include not just the facts but an acquaintance with the affective life of all involved parties. In Christianity as well as Judaism and Islam, God is also understood to be impartial.

If we look just to the features of omniscience of facts, impartiality, and affective incorporation, moral reflection can (I suggest) be understood as our seeking a God's-eye point of view. This view of moral reasoning is customarily called the *ideal observer theory* (IOT). Versions of it may be found in the work of David Hume, Adam Smith, Henry Sidgwick, R.M. Hare, Roderick Firth, Peter Singer, Tom Regan, Tom Carson, and even Immanuel Kant and J.S. Mill.

For supporting documentation for the IOT, I recommend the Blackwell *Companion to Ethics* (Singer 1991). From Mary Midgley's treatment of early ethics to the entries on African, Asian, and early American ethics, there are repeated recourses to seeking impartiality, facts, and affective incorporation. The material is too rich and complex to review here, but I take note of the natural (or intuitive) appeal of the IOT when one takes into account the documented, essentially social nature of humanity and the occasions when companionship and cooperation need to be negotiated. Historical moral disputes have been marred by failure to secure a common background philosophy of the relevant facts (you and I have, say, different views of the individual's relation to family, state, empire, or religion), we may have uneven powers of putting ourselves in the other's shoes, and impartiality can be flawed by either excessive attachment to or detachment from local customs, but I see in the history of ethics a pattern in which ideal knowledge, affective identification, and impartiality are proper goals to pursue.

Let us consider a series of objections and replies.

Objection: The IOT is a historical impersonal point of view. The theory is a view from nowhere. Ethics must be grounded in personal, concrete conditions.

Reply: The IOT sketched here is not a view from *nowhere* but, if you will, a comprehensive view from *everywhere*. Some philosophers worry about the idea of a God's-eye point of view because it may obscure or falsify the way things look from the ground, just as you may have little idea of what a village is like when viewed from a plane at thirty-five thousand feet. The IOT is also *not* a matter of impersonal calculation, but one of personal appraisal, a taking into account of personal, specific circumstances. The IOT goal is to take into account as much as one can the variable concrete conditions for moral deliberation.

In the mid twentieth century there was a dominant portrait of philosophical inquiry as something impersonal. A classic version of this may be found at the end of Bertrand Russell's *A History of Western Philosophy*, where he celebrates an impersonal 'scientific truthfulness'.

> In the welter of conflicting fanaticisms, one of the few unifying
> forces is scientific truthfulness, by which I mean the habit of
> basing our beliefs upon observations and inferences as imper-
> sonal, and as much divested of local and temperamental bias, as
> is possible for human beings.
>
> (Russell 1945, 836)

The IOT defended here is explicitly anchored against bias, but
there is also the explicit claim that moral reflection involves an
affective component that takes seriously local temperaments,
traditions, and personal observations.

Objection: But the theory upholds detachment and disin-
terest as ideals that surely falsify the key components of moral
judgment which involves passion and desire.

Reply: 'Impartiality' is not the same as being dispassionate,
disinterested, or apathetic. When you condemn child molesta-
tion with fierce passion you are not ipso facto partial.
Presumably you believe that an *impartial* assessment of the harms
involved ought to give rise to *passionate, determined* disapproval.

Objection: But impartiality is not an attainable ideal. Even
if there could be an ideal observer (or if God is one), why should
I care?

Reply: I submit that impartiality is easily achieved in a wide
range of cases (who would claim that it is merely bias to think
that skinning and salting babies is wrong?) and that, in the hard
cases, impartiality remains an ideal we may approach, even if we
cannot fully achieve it.

As for the person who does not care, I take the (somewhat
controversial) position that not to care at all about how your acts
affect others, or how they would be viewed from an impartial
point of view, is to court an amoral life. I do not doubt there are
sociopaths or egoistic individuals or societies that promote
egoism on a massive scale. I just doubt whether one can do this
and still claim to be ethical or to reflect ethically.

I suggest that taking into account positions other than one's own is a basic capacity that is evident in much recorded historical moral debate. In fact, finding one's *own* moral point of view (that is, one that you recognize as authentically yours) may be latent and subsequent to grasping the points of view of others. Søren Kierkegaard has taught us that many of us can go through life in an unreflective, routinized fashion, merely accepting the status quo or having alien, destructive points of view forced upon us which then tend to cripple us and those we love. Finding one's own stance can involve an essential comparison of alternative moral positions.

I should also add this caveat: it is in keeping with the IOT developed here that there may be times when the pursuit of objective impartiality may be impossible or dangerous. Imagine you are in a culture where the ostensible objective biology as taught in schools is profoundly racist. The IOT allows us to say that such so-called 'objectivity' is spurious, and that the pursuit of such learning would be noxious. The IOT can allow that, although impartiality is the goal of moral reflection, there are times when a person may not be blameworthy in pursuing impartiality especially when the available resources to achieve impartiality are spurious or unreliable.

At the end of the day, I suggest that the IOT articulated here does more to promote the virtue of humility than the vice of arrogance. Many of those who have struggled to place narrow self-interest to one side (Iris Murdoch, Virginia Woolf, Martin Luther King, Jr, Gandhi) testify to the arduous strain of truly recognizing and responding to the values in and around us without acting upon only our own desires come what may.

Objection: As a final objection, let us look to the underlying rationale for the IOT. I have advanced the theory here as a way to articulate a unified framework to weigh secular and religious values. But religious traditions make specific claims about God's commands. Some believe, for example, that God prohibits homosexual relations between consenting adults in a committed relationship. Others think that such relations are morally permissible. Here we would seem to have a severe collapse of the utility of an IOT in adjudicating contrary claims. Isn't this a case where an idealized God's-eye point of view collides with what persons think is God's actual view? Given such a collision, doesn't the IOT simply fail to bridge religious and secular values?

Reply: I suggest that the most promising reply is to extend a point made in chapter 2 about the biblical God. If a theist has *compelling reasons*, based on impartial and fully informed, affective awareness of all relevant states of affairs, that such same-sex relations are permissible (natural or good) then (on the grounds that God is essentially good) she has reason to believe God does not prohibit same-sex relations. Many Christian homosexuals have taken this approach and argue that apparent divinely revealed precepts prohibiting homosexuality are either not directed at consensual, committed same-sex relations (they are instead directed at homosexual prostitution, homosexual rape, or sexual activity against one's natural sexual orientation, whatever that might be) or the biblical passages are culturally specific and not binding on the future Christian community (like the New Testament injunction against women speaking in church, an injunction most contemporary Christians do not treat as normative today). This stance runs parallel with the way some have treated the Old Testament (or Hebrew Bible) story in which God appears to command Abraham to sacrifice his son, Isaac. Immanuel Kant famously proposed what Abraham should have said upon thinking that God had made such a command:

> Abraham should have replied to this supposedly divine voice: 'That I ought not to kill my good son is quite certain. But that you, this apparition, are God – of that I am not certain, and never can be, not even if this voice rings down to me from (visible) heaven.

> (Kant 1996, 283)

Without delving into the Abraham–Isaac narrative in Genesis 22 (there are ways to interpret the narrative as God instructing Abraham *not* to practice child sacrifice), a theist using the IOT may be convinced on grounds of impartiality etc. that same-sex unions are not ipso facto wrong and that an essentially good God's *apparent* disapproval of such union is more apparent than actual. While some Christians adhere to a strict understanding of biblical authority and sometimes offer independent reasons for disapproving of homosexual activity, others adopt the position I have sketched here.

But although someone may use the IOT to modify what they believe to be authentic divine revelation, there can be ways in which attention to the values found in specific religious traditions ought to have a role in modifying one's search for comprehensive impartiality. I advance four areas in which religious values may well have a claim on such broader ethical reflection. But before I do so let us consider secular and religious values in ethics.

Ethics and evidence

When addressing a string of theistic arguments in chapter 3, I noted that some theists question the need for evidence to back up one's religious convictions. Could it be that religious convictions (theistic or non-theistic) arise naturally and might well be warranted even if no independent case supports them? W.K. Clifford (1845–79) famously argued that it is always wrong to believe anything without sufficient evidence. Philosophers have sometimes insisted that if we are unable to ground our beliefs in compelling, available evidence we should withhold our assent and remain agnostic.

It is difficult to arrive at a consensus of what should constitute *sufficient evidence* when assessing philosophical worldviews. Clifford never defined 'sufficient evidence', though he offered a colorful illustration of acting wrongly on the grounds of insufficient evidence.

> A shipowner was about to send to sea an emigrant-ship. He knew that she was old, and not overwell built at the first; that she had seen many seas and climes, and often had needed repairs. Doubts had been suggested to him that possibly she was not seaworthy. These doubts preyed upon his mind, and made him unhappy; he thought that perhaps he ought to have her thoroughly overhauled and refitted, even though this should put him at great expense. Before the ship sailed, however, he succeeded in overcoming these melancholy reflections. He said to himself that she had gone safely through so many voyages and weathered so many storms that it was idle to suppose she would not come safely home from this trip also. The shipowner becomes convinced (or self-deceived?) in the belief that the ship is safe and when it sinks with no survivors, he goes to collect the insurance money with a clean conscience.

> (Clifford 1947, 70)

This is a great case of negligence or recklessness and Clifford's conclusion seems sound. But it is one thing to have standards of evidence that are stable and a matter of common sense when it comes to launching ships or spacecrafts, building bridges, and so on; what standards should be employed when launching or embracing worldviews? The five world religions are old, but so are naturalism and skepticism. Naturalism and skepticism may or may not have been built well initially, and both have sometimes needed repair. Buddhism needs to address difficulties from its no-self philosophy and theistic religions need to address the problem of evil. Skepticism itself faces many challenges. For example, there are radical forms of skepticism that appear to be self-contradictory, e.g. a person claims to know that no one knows anything, or a person claims to be a radical skeptic but in practice the person must act as a non-skeptic, and so on. Would Cliffordian standards outlaw virtually all the major philosophical positions, including his own (he has no general argument that we need to have sufficient evidence that we should never have a belief without sufficient evidence)?

One of the more interesting replies to Clifford was developed by William James (1842–1910). James contended that circumstances may arise when we face a non-trivial choice between live, incompatible hypotheses (neither is known to be false and each has some credibility) and we seem to have no alternative but to believe (accept or assume) one of them. There may be overriding reasons in terms of value to accept one hypothesis over the other. James contended that in matters of religion or spirituality as well as when it comes to believing we have freedom or are determined, we are entitled to accept some beliefs (and practices) because of their value, e.g. they help foster compassion or a sense of fulfillment, they may provide living contact with God, and so on (James 1956, 28–30). James is in the tradition of Blaise Pascal (1623–62), who argued that if the reasons for and against God's existence were evenly matched, we should wager that God exists.

There seems, in principle, nothing *obviously* wrong with taking values seriously when making momentous decisions under conditions of uncertainty. In an emergency you may have to rely on a mere hunch in choosing alternatives. What you believe may not be under your voluntary control (e.g. it would be difficult to believe there are unicorns without evidence, even if you were offered great wealth for such an act of belief), but something approaching belief seems possible to achieve even when the evidence is quite thin. I might, for example, live and act as though a friend is faithful even in the face of some counter-evidence, e.g. rumors of betrayal. What seems evident, however, is that any full use of Jamesian reasoning will need to take as comprehensive a view of the relevant values as possible. It is open (I suggest) in principle for a theist to follow James in arguing for the great benefits of theistic life and practice, but then it should be open for the naturalist to argue for the benefits of the life of a naturalist, and for a Buddhist to make a case for the fulfillment available through Buddhism. There are even philosophical traditions of skepticism that have been advanced on the grounds that skepticism fosters a good life that is free from the ills of passion.

Although I see no reason to put Jamesian reasoning out of bounds, historically it seems that philosophy as a practice has largely challenged the legitimacy of a belief or worldview simply on grounds it offers contentment or convenience. Recall the point made in chapter 1 about the roots of philosophy in its confrontations with the status quo. (Perhaps the best balance of values and the pursuit of cognition or knowledge is the Hindu and Buddhist model sketched in the last chapter.)

I end this chapter by noting three areas where you may wish to further investigate religious values and their possible role in ethical inquiry. Because the purpose of this book is to enable the *beginning* of inquiry, rather than the end, I present these cases in terms of questions for further inquiry in developing a comprehensive ethic.

Three domains of value in religious ethics

The importance of ritual

Current ethical secular theory pays very little attention to ritual. A look at Chinese philosophy of religion would prompt one to reconsider the value of rites. Why is it that Confucianism flourished while the contemporary movement of Moism with its teaching of universal love did not? The teachings of Mo Tzu in the fifth century are deeply attractive and would resonate with those who endorse impartialist ethics, but they lacked the deep anchorage that Confucianism had in ritual practice. Although the stress on rites can be exaggerated (Taoists historically critiqued rites as leading to empty acts), the comparative success of Confucianism is a sign that rites can have an enduring role in moral, religious, and personal formation.

Cross-generational values

An appreciation of African religious ethics would challenge the current tendency to neglect the wisdom of the elderly and to focus instead on youth and technology. In 'Differentiations in African Ethics', Bénézet Bujo offers this portrait of sub-Saharan African values:

In modern society, particularly in the West, young people no longer seem to be interested in the elderly other than as a burden to get rid of. Advertising praises eternal youth. As everything centers on profitability, the elderly are relegated to oblivion and anonymity, since they prove unable to perform as society requires.

The value of African tradition could usefully be reasserted here. In Africa the elderly are treated with great respect, and by virtue of their long experience are considered a source of wisdom. Even if they are no longer able to generate or bear biological life, they continue to strengthen and increase the life of the whole community through their great wisdom. When one talks of teaching through experience, it is not at all about transmitting technological knowledge, for instance, because younger people can be experts on this. The experience African tradition talks about is at a more existential level; this experi- ence is what provides technology itself with its soul, so that it is not know-how devoid of wisdom. A technology devoid of wisdom is dehumanizing and leads to death. From the African point of view, a society that dispenses with the experience of

the elderly ruins itself because it will not be able to identify the
forces of life and death in the cosmos.

(Bujo 2005, 434–5)

Non-violence

In our current violent world and prevailing assumption that
deadly violence can be warranted, it is worth taking seriously
religious movements of non-violence. An ethic of strict non-
violence today has been attacked by various philosophers (most
prominently Jan Narveson) on the grounds of being either
irrational or unethical. If the only way you could prevent a
malicious gunman from killing ten innocent people is by killing
him, and you do not do so, then ceteris paribus you are partly
responsible for these deaths. Moreover, your not taking the life of
the gunman may cause us to question whether you honestly do
think killing is a grave wrong. After all, if killing is a grave wrong,
shouldn't one seek to minimize killing, and if the only way to do
so is by your killing one person to save ten, shouldn't you do so?

This critique of a non-violent ethic may or may not be
successful. Arguably, the critique rests on a form of utilitarianism
and a notion that the end justifies the means. But I think the
above critique has force unless one has a background belief
in the sacred such as we find in Jainism and its reverence for life
principle or Gandhi's Hinduism in divine commands such as
Christian pacifists believe they find in the teachings of Jesus. A
fruitful, more comprehensive account of the value and rigor of
an ethic of non-violence needs to take seriously both a secular
and a religious case for non-violence.

An exploration of religious ethics in these and other areas can
enrich secular ethical theory. A deeper background in such
religious ethical practices may also aid one in cross-cultural and
religious dialogue.

Conclusion and resources for further work

I hope that in reading this book you have (whatever your own religious commitments, if any) seen good reasons to engage philosophically with both religious and secular values and beliefs. At its best, the philosophy of religion is about openness to serious dialogue and respectful argument across religious, cultural, and other boundaries. The kind of careful, disciplined thinking we have discussed provides one of the best ways to engage other religions, and to engage those who reject religion, in a way that can bring deeper understanding of and sympathy for others.

Philosophy of religion today is carried out in a host of contexts: conferences, journals, undergraduate and graduate courses, philosophy clubs, institutes dedicated to philosophy of religion, books, and websites, as well as in coffee houses, homes, and anywhere else friends can talk together about the things that interest them. Most of the major publishing houses have books on the philosophy of religion, including anthologies of classical and contemporary works. The free online *Stanford Encyclopedia of Philosophy* contains some brilliant articles on some of the major contributors to and themes in philosophy of religion.

After reading enough of the literature to understand the kinds of issues professional philosophers address, you may wish to begin attending meetings on philosophy of religion. You can find access to these through the American Philosophical Association, the American Academy of Religion, the British Society for Philosophy of Religion, the Canadian Philosophical Association, the Australasian Association of Philosophy, or the philosophical association in other countries. Subscribing to journals in the field is a great way to access the very latest developments and to begin reflecting on how you might contribute. I highly recommend these outstanding journals: *Religious Studies*, *Faith and Philosophy*, the *International Journal for Philosophy of Religion*, *Sophia*, *Philosophia Christi*, and *Ars Disputandi*. The last journal is online and free, whereas the others require subscriptions. Your nearby university or college is likely to have access to most of them, and specific articles of interest may be ordered online. Mainstream philosophy journals such as *Mind*, *Philosophy*, *American Philosophical Quarterly*, and *Philosophical Quarterly* all carry articles on philosophy of religion, as well as in other areas. The free online journal *Notre Dame Philosophical Review* carries regular reviews of work in philosophy of religion. Oxford University Press, Cambridge University Press, Blackwell–Wiley, and Routledge offer excellent companions to the philosophy of religion. I have co-edited the first edition of the Blackwell *Companion to Philosophy of Religion* with Philip Quinn (1997) and am co-editing the second edition with Paul Draper (forthcoming). Acumen will be publishing a five-volume work, *A History of Western Philosophy of Religion*, edited by Graham Oppy and Nick Trakakis. This promises to be definitive as a resource as well as a superb collection of writing by diverse leading contributors to philosophy of religion today. I have written a history of philosophy of religion in modern philosophy entitled *Evidence and Faith: Philosophy of Religion since the Seventeenth Century* (2005b).

Two especially active centers for philosophy of religion can be explored online for upcoming events and opportunities: the Center for Philosophy of Religion at the University of Notre

Dame (US), which attracts leading philosophers of religion and hosts various lectures, and the Centre of Theology and Philosophy at the University of Nottingham (UK), which hosts annual conferences.

If you are interested in corresponding about any of the themes covered in this introduction or other themes that emerge in your research and reflections, please feel free to contact me.

Charles Taliaferro
Department of Philosophy
St Olaf College
1520 St Olaf Avenue
Northfield, MN 55057
USA
<taliafer@stolaf.edu>

Bibliography

Adams, M.M. 1990. 'Horrendous Evils and the Goodness of God.' In *The Problem of Evil*, ed. M.M. and R.M. Adams. Oxford, Oxford University Press

—— 1999. *Horrendous Evils and the Goodness of God*. Ithaca, NY, Cornell University Press

Adams, R.M. 1993. 'Religious Ethics in a Pluralist Society.' In *Prospects for a Common Morality*, ed. G. Outka and J.P. Reeder. Princeton, NJ, Princeton University Press

Aquinas, T. 1947. *Summa Theologica*. New York, Benzinger

Audi, R. 1989. 'The Separation of Church and State and the Obligations of Citizenship.' *Philosophy and Public Affairs*, 18, pp. 259–96

Augustine. 1972 [426]. *The City of God*, trans. H. Bettenson. Harmondsworth, England, Penguin

—— 1991 [430]. *Confessions*, trans. H. Chadwick. Oxford, Oxford University Press

Avila, C. 1983. *Ownership: Early Christian Teachings*. London, Sheed & Ward

Bagger, M. 1999. *Religious Experience, Justification, and History*. Cambridge, England, Cambridge University Press

Baker, L.R. 2000. *Persons and Bodies*. Cambridge, England, Cambridge University Press

—— 2005. 'Death and the Afterlife.' In *The Oxford Handbook of Philosophy of Religion*, ed. W. Wainwright. Oxford, Oxford University Press

Berger, P.L. 1997. 'Epistemological Modesty: An Interview with Peter Berger.' *Christian Century*, 14, pp. 972–5

Bertocci, P. 1970. *The Person God Is*. London, Allen & Unwin

Blanshard, B. 1958. 'The Case for Determinism.' In *Determinism and Freedom*, ed. S. Hook. New York, New York University Press

Brody, B. 1974. 'Morality and Religion Reconsidered.' In *Readings in the Philosophy of Religion: An Analytical Approach*, ed. B. Brody. Englewood Cliffs, NJ, Prentice Hall

Bujo, B. 2005. 'Differentiations in African Ethics.' In *The Blackwell Companion to Religious Ethics*, ed. W. Schweiker. Oxford, Blackwell

Clack, B. and Clack, B. 2008. *The Philosophy of Religion: A Critical Introduction*, 2nd edn. Cambridge, England, Polity Press

Clifford, W.K. 2006 [1901]. *Lectures and Essays*. Read Books

Cohn-Sherbok, D. 1990. 'Jewish Faith and the Holocaust.' *Religious Studies*, 26(2), pp. 267–75

Craig, W.L. and Smith, Q. 1993. *Theism, Atheism, and Big Bang Cosmology*. Oxford, Clarendon Press

Cupitt, D. 1981. *Taking Leave of God*. New York, Crossroad

Darwin, C. 2002 [1876]. *Autobiographies*. Harmondsworth, England, Penguin

Davies, B. 2004. *An Introduction to the Philosophy of Religion*. Oxford, Oxford University Press

—— 2006. *The Reality of God and the Problem of Evil*. London, Continuum

Dawkins, R. 2006. *The God Delusion*. Boston, Houghton Mifflin

de Chardin, P.T. 2002. *Christianity and Evolution*, trans. R. Hague. New York, Harcourt

Dennett, D. 2006. *Breaking the Spell*. New York, Viking

Eckel, M.D. 2007. 'Responsibility without a Self.' In *Responsibility*, ed. B. Darling-Smith. Lanham, MD, Lexington Books

Edwards, P. 1974. 'The Cosmological Argument.' In *Readings in the Philosophy of Religion: An Analytical Approach*, ed. B. Brody. Englewoods Cliffs, NJ, Prentice Hall.

Evans, S. 1985. *Philosophy of Religion*. Downers Grove, IL, Intervarsity

Ewing, A.C. 1985. *The Fundamental Questions of Philosophy*. London, Routledge & Kegan Paul

Goetz, S. and Taliaferro, C. 2008. *Naturalism (Interventions)*. Grand Rapids, MI, Eerdmans

Goodman, L. 1995. 'Jewish Philosophy.' In *The Oxford Companion to Philosophy*, ed. T. Honderich. Oxford, Oxford University Press

Halbfass, W. 2003. 'Darsana, Anviksiki, Philosophy.' In *Philosophy of Religion: An Anthology*, ed. C. Taliaferro and P.J. Griffiths. Malden, MA, Blackwell

Harris, S. 2004. *The End of Faith: Religion, Terror, and the Future of Unreason*. New York, W.W. Norton

Haskar, V. 1991. *Indivisible Selves and Moral Practice*. New York, Barnes & Noble Books

Hasker, W. 2008. *The Triumph of God over Evil*. Downers Grove, IL, IVP

Heim, M. 2005. 'Differentiations in Hindu Ethics'. In *The Blackwell Companion to Religious Ethics*, ed. W. Schweiker. Malden, MA, Blackwell

Hick, J. 1977. 'Jesus and World Religions.' In *The Myth of God Incarnate*, ed. J. Hick. London, SCM

—— 1978. *Evil and the God of Love*. New York, Harper & Row

—— 2000. 'Religious Pluralism and Salvation.' In *The Philosophical Challenge of Religious Diversity*, ed. P.L. Quinn and K. Meeker. Oxford, Oxford University Press

Hiriyanna, M. 1951. *The Essentials of Indian Philosophy*. Delhi, Motilal Banarsidass

Hirsch, E. 1993. *Dividing Reality*. Oxford, Oxford University Press

Holt, J.C. 1981. 'Assisting the Dead by Venerating the Living: Merit Transfer in the Early Buddhist Tradition.' *Numen*, 28(1), pp. 1–28

Honderich, T., ed. 1995. 'Materialism.' In *The Oxford Companion to Philosophy*. Oxford, Oxford University Press

Hume, D. 1902. 'Enquiry Concerning Human Understanding.' In *Hume Enquiries*, ed. D. Selby-Bigge. Oxford, Oxford University Press

—— 1976. *The Natural History of Religion and Dialogues Concerning Nature*, ed. J. V. Price. Oxford, Clarendon Press

Idziak, J., ed. 1980. *Divine Command Morality: Historical and Contemporary Readings*. New York, Edwin Mellen

James, W. 1956. *The Will to Believe and Other Essays in Popular Philosophy*. New York, Dover

—— 1960 [1902]. *Varieties of Religious Experience*. Glasgow, Fontana

Jantzen, G. 1979. 'Hume on Miracles, History, and Politics.' *Christian Scholars Review*, 8(4), pp. 318–25

—— 1984. 'Do We Need Immortality?' *Modern Theology*, 1(1), pp. 33–44

Kane, S.G. 1975. 'The Failure of Soul-Making Theodicy.' *International Journal for the Philosophy of Religion*, 6(1), pp. 1–22

Kant, I. 1950 [1781]. *Critique of Pure Reason*. London, Macmillan

—— 1996. *Religion within the Boundaries of Mere Reason*, ed. A.W. Wood and G. di Giovanni. Cambridge, England: Cambridge University Press

Kenny, A. 1979. *The God of the Philosophers*. Oxford, Clarendon Press

—— 1992. *What Is Faith?* Oxford, Oxford University Press

Koller, J. 1985. *Oriental Philosophies*. New York, Charles Scribner's Sons

Leftow, B. 1991. *Time and Eternity*. Ithaca, NY, Cornell University Press

Lewis, C.S. 1992. *An Experiment in Criticism*. Cambridge, England, Cambridge University Press

Lewis, H.D. 1959. *Our Experience of God*. New York, Macmillan

Lockwood, M. 2003. 'Consciousness and the Quantum World: Putting Qualia on the Map.' In *Consciousness: New Philosophical Perspectives*, ed. Q. Smith and A. Jokic. Oxford, Clarendon Press

Lombardi, J. 1984. 'Suicide and the Service of God.' *Ethics*, 95, pp. 56–67

Macedo, S. 1993. 'Toleration and Fundamentalism.' In *A Companion to Contemporary Political Philosophy*, ed. R. Goodin and P. Pettit. Oxford, Basil Blackwell

Mackie, J.L. 1983. *The Miracle of Theism*. Oxford, Clarendon Press

Malalasekera, G.P. 1967. 'Transference of Merit in Ceylonese Buddhism.' *Philosophy East and West*, 17, pp. 85–90

Martin, M. 1990. *Atheism*. Philadelphia, Temple University Press

Mavrodes, G. 1986. 'Religion and the Queerness of Morality.' In *Rationality, Religious Belief and Moral Commitment*, ed. R. Audi and W. Wainwright. Ithaca, NY, Cornell University Press

McGinn, C. 1990. *The Problems of Consciousness*. Oxford, Basil Blackwell

Merricks, T. 1999. 'The Resurrection of the Body and the Life Everlasting.' In *Reasons for the Hope Within*, ed. M. Murray. Grand Rapids, MI, Eerdmans

—— 2001. 'How to Live Forever without Saving Your Soul: Physicalism and Immortality.' In *Soul, Body, and Survival*, ed. K. Corcoran. Ithaca, NY, Cornell University Press

Modée, J. *Artifacts and Supraphysical Words: A Conceptual Analysis of Religion*. Lund, Sweden, Lund University Press

Monius, A.E. 2005. 'Origins of Hindu Ethics.' In *The Blackwell Companion to Religious Ethics*, ed. W. Schweiker. Malden, MA, Blackwell

Narveson, J. 2003. 'God by Design?' In *God and Design: The Teleological Argument and Modern Science*, ed. N.A. Manson. London, Routledge

O'Connor, T. 2008. *Theism and Ultimate Explanation: The Necessary Shape of Contingency*. Oxford, Blackwell

O'Hear, A. 1984. *Experience, Explanation, and Faith: An Introduction to the Philosophy of Religion*. London, Routledge & Kegan Paul

Owen, H.P. 1965. *The Moral Argument for Christian Theism*. London, George Allen & Unwin

Peterson, M., ed. 1992. *The Problem of Evil*. Notre Dame, IN, University of Notre Dame Press

Phillips, D.Z. 2007. 'Four Philosophers out of Practice.' *Philosophia Christi*, 9(2), pp. 297–312

Plantinga, A. 2008. *The Knowledge of God*. Oxford, Oxford University Press

Radhakrishnan, S. 1936. 'Spirit in Man.' In *Contemporary Indian Philosophy*, trans. J.J. Muirhead. London, George Allen & Unwin

—— 1960. *The Brahma Sutra*. New York, Harper

—— and Moore, C.A., eds. 1967. *A Sourcebook in Indian Philosophy*. Princeton, NJ, Princeton University Press

Rawls, J. 1993. *Political Liberalism*. New York, Columbia University Press

Reichenbach, B. 1990. *The Law of Karma*. Honolulu, University of Hawaii Press

Rolston III, H. 2003. 'Does Nature Need to Be Redeemed?' In *Philosophy of Religion: An Anthology*, ed. C. Taliaferro and P.J. Griffiths. Malden, MA, Blackwell

Rosenthal, D.M. 1998. 'Objections to Dualism.' In *Routledge Encyclopedia of Philosophy*, ed. E. Craig. London, Routledge

Rowe, W. 2003. 'The Problem of Evil and Some Varieties of Atheism.' In *Philosophy of Religion: An Anthology*, ed. C. Taliaferro and P.J. Griffiths. Malden, MA, Blackwell

Ruse, M. 1989, *The Darwinian Paradigm*. London, Routledge

Russell, B. 1945. *History of Western Philosophy*. New York, Simon & Schuster

—— 1957. *The Existence of God. A Debate between B. Russell and F.C. Copleston. Why I Am Not a Christian*. London, Allen & Unwin

Schellenberg, J. 2007. *The Wisdom to Doubt*. Ithaca, NY, Cornell University Press

Shankara, 1970. *Shankara's Crest Jewel of Discrimination*, trans. Swaimi Prabhavanda and C. Isherwood. New York, Mentor Books

Singer, P., ed. 1991. *A Companion to Ethics*. Oxford, Blackwell

Soelle, D. 1984. *The Strength of the Weak*. Philadelphia, Westminster Press.

Sorenson, R. 1992. *Thought Experiments*. Oxford, Oxford University Press.

Stark, R. 2006. Economics of Religion. In *The Blackwell Companion to the Study of Religion*, ed. R. Segal. Oxford, Blackwell

Suzuki, D.T. 1933. *Essays in Zen Buddhism*. London, Luzac

Swinburne, R. 1993. *The Coherence of Theism*. Oxford, Oxford University Press

—— 1996. *Is There a God?*. Oxford, Oxford University Press

Taliaferro, C. 2005a. *Consciousness and the Mind of God*. Cambridge, England, Cambridge University Press

—— 2005b. *Evidence and Faith: Philosophy of Religion since the Seventeenth Century*. Cambridge, England, Cambridge University Press

—— and Tepley, A. 2005. *Cambridge Platonist Spirituality*. Mahwah, NJ, Paulist Press.

Taylor, R. 1974. *Metaphysics*, 3rd edn. Englewood Cliffs, NJ, Prentice Hall

van Inwagen, P. 1998. *The Possibility of Resurrection and Other Essays in Christian Apologetics*. Boulder, CO, Westview Press

—— 2003. 'The Problem of Evil, the Problem of Air, and the Problem of Silence.' In *Philosophy of Religion: An Anthology*, ed. C. Taliaferro and P.J. Griffiths. Malden, MA, Blackwell

Waldron, J. 1987. 'Theoretical Foundations of Liberalism.' *Philosophical Quarterly*, 37, pp. 109–25

Ward, K. 2000. 'Truth and the Diversity of Religions.' In *The Philosophical Challenge of Religious Diversity*, ed. P.L. Quinn & K. Meeker. Oxford, Oxford University Press

Wettstein, H. 1997. 'Awe and the Religious Life.' In *Philosophy of Religion*, ed. P. French et al. Notre Dame, IN, University of Notre Dame Press

Wollstonecraft, M. 1996. *A Vindication of the Rights of Women*. Mineola, NY, Dover

Yandell, K. 1984. *Christianity and Philosophy*. Grand Rapids, MI, Eerdmans

Young, R. 1977. 'Theism and Morality.' *Canadian Journal of Philosophy*, 7(2), pp. 341–52

Zimmerman, D. 2003. 'Christians Should Affirm Mind–Body Dualism.' In *Contemporary Debates in the Philosophy of Religion*, ed. M.L. Peterson and R.J. Vanarragon. Oxford, Blackwell

Index